DISTRACTED

UN

DISTRACTED

UN

Capture Your Purpose
Rediscover Your Joy

BOB GOFF

NELSON
BOOKS

An Imprint of Thomas Nelson

Published in Nashville, Tennessee, by Nelson Books, an imprint of Thomas Nelson. Nelson Books and Thomas Nelson are registered trademarks of HarperCollins Christian Publishing, Inc.

Represented by Alive Literary Agency, www.aliveliterary.com.

Thomas Nelson titles may be purchased in bulk for educational, business, fundraising, or sales promotional use. For information, please e-mail SpecialMarkets@ThomasNelson.com.

ISBN 978-1-4002-2811-9 (eBook)
ISBN 978-1-4002-2697-9 (HC)
ISBN 978-1-4002-3535-3 (IE)

Library of Congress Control Number: 2021951286

Printed in the United States of America
22 23 24 25 26 LSC 10 9 8 7 6 5 4 3 2 1

*This book is dedicated to Sweet Maria Goff
and our expanding family.
Thank you Lindsey, Jon, Richard, Ashley, Adam, and
Kaitlyn, you are my teachers and I'm your biggest fan.
Most of what I have ever written down in a book I learned
from simply watching you live your beautiful lives.
G. K. Chesterton once told his friends, "I'm sorry for
the long letter, I didn't have time to write a short one."
This book is the long letter you have helped me write to
myself about the kind of undistracted life I strive to have.
The model of your lives is pointing the way for me.*

---

*I also dedicate these words to my friend Bill Lokey, who gave
away extravagant love to me while fighting a courageous battle
against cancer. Thank you for teaching me not to be fearful
or distracted about what happens after this life ends . . . and
for the promise that arriving in heaven will be simply like
stepping from the boat to the dock. Welcome ashore, Bill.*

---

*And finally, to everyone who forgot about the important work
they were called to do because they were distracted by what
seemed more urgent, even if it wasn't. My hope is that these pages
will help you find your way back to the big and undistracted life
Jesus invited you to live. Be relentless in your efforts to locate
this place; do whatever it takes to get there. Once you arrive,
don't let anything but heaven cause you to budge from it.*

CONTENTS

CHAPTER 1

THE DESTRUCTION
OF DISTRACTION

*Living on purpose is like a
horse wearing blinders.*

A couple of years ago I traveled with a few friends to Kurdistan, a place near Iran's border. We had started a school in the region and were building a hospital and housing for refugees. One morning we got up early and went to the top of a mountain that divided Iraq and Iran. It was a rocky and nondescript area. I remembered from a decade ago when three Americans were taken into custody by Iranian border guards for crossing into Iran while hiking on this mountain. I understood how easy it could be to get confused about what side of a border you were on. A line on a map doesn't always translate to markings on the ground.

As I walked with my friends, we saw a sign indicating a minefield separating the two countries. *This must be the border,* I thought. I

1

couldn't read the language on the sign, but the skull, crossbones, and drawing of an explosion told the story pretty clearly. I decided to throw a couple of rocks into the minefield to see if anything would happen. I know, I know, it probably wasn't such a great idea, but it was the best bad idea I could come up with at the time. After ten or fifteen minutes I looked over at the landmine sign again and noticed it had been dug up. We weren't on the perimeter throwing rocks *into* the minefield; it was just as likely that we were *in* the minefield.

Be honest. From time to time we all find ourselves in dangerous places when we think we are safe. Distraction is what leads us into this kind of minefield. No matter who you are, somehow or somewhere you will cross over and find yourself in the middle of something you thought you were only adjacent to or on the edge of.

You and I need to recognize the signs that we are becoming distracted. While we might notice our minds wandering, we also need to look at the meandering nature of our activities. Rather than making decisions consistent with who God says we are, we might be acting like the person someone else wants us to be. Perhaps comparison is leading you away from yourself. Maybe it is financial pressures or deep-seated insecurities or past failures that are overly influencing your present decisions. We need to recognize these things in our lives before we can begin the courageous work of moving forward.

Try this: Take some notes for an entire day on how you are spending time between the big projects or commitments in your life. Don't just write down "I worked on writing my paper today" or "I spent the day preparing for my weekend trip." Write down all the things that distracted you from writing or preparing that day. Again, be honest: "I went to the post office. I chased the neighbor's dog out of my yard. I compared my failure with someone else's success. I ate a Pop-Tart." Keep it real and admit you had three. Distractions like these make up the minefield you are in right now, not the one you think you are still on the perimeter of. A thousand such unnoticed distractions are getting in the way of your joy and preventing you from living with the kind of focused purpose that will produce the life you are longing for.

Don't feel bad about all the things that have been grabbing your attention. We all become distracted at some point. It is somehow built into our operating systems. We become distracted from our goals and greater purposes by our temporary circumstances. We can be distracted by each other and even away from God and what we really believe to be true. Sadly, the boatload of goodness we could bring to the world is being scuttled by the many things that carry us so far away from the dock we can no longer make the leap back to shore. We get stuck in the past, worry about the present, or get distracted by the future. We no longer lean into our lives right where we are but instead lean away from them and become individuals who bear little resemblance to the people God intended us to become.

I started a retreat center called The Oaks with some friends in Southern California and was filming a series with a fun and really creative group of people. They explained to me that they had a final closing scene in mind where they would fly a couple of cameras in by drone and capture me holding a bunch of balloons while standing on top of the sixty-foot-tall water tower on the property. All I needed to do was climb to the top. It sounded like another really dangerous idea, so we got started with the preparations right away. The water tower is on a big hill covered in waist-high brush, and we took a small road to the top with dozens of brightly colored helium balloons held out the windows.

When I got to the base of the water tower, I looked up at the dozens of rungs leading upward. This wasn't going to be easy. The wind was blowing pretty hard, and as I looked up I was completely engrossed in counting the rungs, planning my moves, and thinking about how I could get myself and the balloons up to the top in one piece. If I fell, at least I could land on the balloons, right? I continued to stand at the base of the tower for a few long minutes, looking up and puzzling together all the details I thought would be necessary to navigate my way upward. For no particular reason, I broke from my upward stare, glanced down, and discovered a coiled rattlesnake at my feet. *Yikes!*

Had I been bitten, this would be a much better story. I wondered whether I was flexible enough to get my ankle up to my face so I could suck the venom out. I'm not going to lie; it would have been quite a power yoga move. I slowly backed away, thankful I wouldn't have to pull a hamstring to save my own life. This episode got me thinking. Sometimes we are so busy looking up and looking forward trying to figure out the next moves in our lives—or looking backward at all the places we have been—that we don't look down and figure out where we actually are.

In a sense, we have all been bitten by something just as poisonous as that rattlesnake: the massive number of distractions around us. We live much of our lives struggling for focus, unsure of how to interact with our family or friends. We fret about our popularity and our faith. We question our college majors and career choices. Sometimes married couples wonder about their choices too. *Did I pick the right person? Am I the right person? Who changed? Me? You? Both of us? And what do we do now?*

No wonder we're confused. We arrive as babies, placed in the arms of parents who are complete amateurs with no owner's manual and usually no clue how to raise us. Most of us start broke or broken, and some of us stay that way. Some strike it rich but then accumulate a distorted view of their wealth; still others never find healing in their search for wholeness. Add to this that we're following a God we can't see, for a lifetime we can't measure, to a heaven we can't comprehend, because of grace we didn't earn. Again, is it any wonder we're all a little muddled?

In truth, we are all trying to build the airplane while flying it—figuring it out as we go. This means more off-ramps than on-ramps, more chances for confusion than certainty, and more ambiguity than clarity. In a word, much of life can leave us feeling completely, inextricably, absolutely, and totally *distracted*. When this happens, one of the first casualties is our joy.

All this vagueness plays right into the hands of darkness too. I am not prone to seeing the devil around every corner, but I am starting to see he has got a clever ploy. I don't think he wants to destroy us with an obvious, all-out frontal assault. No, I think evil wants to distract us from expressing our gifts and doing what we are meant to do. Darkness is rarely content to wound us with one decisive blow when it can injure us equally with a thousand paper cuts. Honestly, it seems like evil has been doing a pretty good job of keeping us out of the fight and entangled in the ropes of distraction.

You know those indentations they put on the sides of the highway, the ones that go *guh-guh-guh-guh-guh* if you drift out of the lane? Those are called "rumble strips." I want this book to be like a rumble strip in your life. Listen: You are on a path. You're going places. I don't care whether you drive NASCAR or are waiting for your driver's permit; it's common to drift every once in a while. And not the cool kind of drift you see in the movies or on TikTok—the bad kind that will leave you overturned in a ditch. This book will give you a few ideas about how to yank back into your lane, refocus, get clear once again on your lasting purposes, and start living a less distracted and more joy-filled life right now. No one asks for permission to stay on the road; and you don't need permission to live your life either. Just decide right now that you are going to lean into the rich, meaningful, beautiful, oftentimes painful life God has already given you.

We all know someone who won't pull over and ask for directions. I used to be one of them, and I think I now know why. Most of us don't want to be told what to do, even when it would be helpful to us. The fact is, we don't need more information; we need more examples. Stay close to a few people who understand how to resist distraction and direct their energy toward their most lasting purposes, and some of this intentionality will rub off on you. Imagine what could happen if you focused your attention on what really matters instead of all the things that don't. What an amazing example of love, purpose, and joy you would be to countless others. These are the things both simple lives and grand legends are made of.

Let's be honest with each other. There is a lot of second-best available to all of us. If we aren't aware of the alternatives, we won't realize we are settling for less than what is accessible to us. This book won't tell you what to think or what to do, but I hope it reminds you about who you already are. You are someone who has permission to live with an unreasonable, unthinkable, totally absurd amount of focus, purpose, joy, and fulfillment.

Here are a few questions I have for you as we begin this journey. Are you willing to do what it takes to uncover the wonder that already surrounds your life? Will you do the courageous work to identify what is distracting you from the better things? And finally, are you willing to do the difficult and selfless work of releasing the beauty you discover into the lives of others rather than keeping it for yourself?

Pulling this off will require us to put on blinders. Like a racehorse in the Kentucky Derby or a dog with a funnel around its neck after going to the vet. We need to block our view of the things that hardly matter at all, stop returning to the patterns that do not serve our larger objectives, start recognizing what is temporary and transitory, and instead focus intensely on the things that will last forever: our faith, our families, and our purposes. When you direct your attention to these things, you will find your joy.

———

If you've read any of my other books, you know I've been focused on Sweet Maria since the moment I saw her. She has captivated me for decades, and she still does. It's easy to stay undistracted when she's around. Of my countless quirks, one thing I do is sing to Sweet Maria every morning. I won't tell you what my repertoire is, but I will say that I am *horrible* at singing. Just plain awful. Think of nails-on-a-chalkboard but goofier, with more arm waving and deeper baritone. It's like a bad Disney tune sung in the key of a dog howling at the moon.

When I sing to Sweet Maria each morning, she usually groans and pulls a pillow over her head. I've told her it's part of the platinum package she got when she said yes to me. She has asked me a few times to downgrade to the aluminum or cardboard packages. You know, the ones that don't include a predawn serenade. I've told her we're all sold out. I know deep down somewhere she loves it. I keep singing my awful songs because they remind me who I am and who I love. The songs remind me first thing each day about the center of my life—our family—which is more important to me than anything except my faith. More important than the reminder, these songs are declarations of what I'm going to do about my priorities. Howling through the new verses I make up each morning, I let Sweet Maria, myself, and the world know what my plan is for the day, and then I endeavor to live it out as best I can.

My hope is that this book will help you find your song or help you sing it a little louder if you already know it. I want my words in these pages to knock loose a couple of verses for you that are filled with love and intention and hope and purpose and Jesus. Maybe it's time for you to hum a few bars each morning about the beautiful life you have been given, the short period of time you have to live it, and the people you could impact if you let your love and creativity off the leash rather than tying it to the past.

This book isn't filled with fables. Instead, it's wall-to-wall with stories. Why? It's simple. Because Jesus told stories. In fact, Scripture says He never spoke to anyone without telling them a couple of good stories to illustrate the truths He wanted to pass along. Stories not only tell us truth but they can also point us toward living lives that are more true. Falsehoods are designed to distract us with deceit; truth, on the other hand, informs and guides us down a brave and more lasting path.

This book is not full of miscellaneous facts either. I've never had a bunch of random, disconnected facts combine into something that changed my life. These days, though, it seems like the world is full to the brim with information. We are drowning in the stuff. On average, human knowledge is doubling every thirteen months, but this deluge of information doesn't provide any more clarity about our lives. To the contrary, it sometimes feels like the facts become a smoke screen lingering between us and the clarity we truly need. Have you noticed that even when facts seem indisputable, people still find a way to spend a weird amount of time arguing about them? Culturally, I think we all sense that we're a little uptight and feisty right now.

Are you willing to accept for a moment that all this noise is a distraction? I am not suggesting that we opt for lives of ignorance. Far from it. Facts can be helpful, but rarely are they *soulful*. We don't need more facts to find the purpose and kindness and unselfishness we long for; we need a firmly seated faith, a few good friends, and a couple of trustworthy reminders. I hope these stories help you sort out what you believe and why. I want this book to nudge you in the direction of who you are becoming rather than leave you wrapped around the axle of who you have been. Because when you and I are laser-focused and clearheaded, I promise we will find our purpose every time. Find your purpose, and you will experience more joy. The math is simple.

Remember, the delight of darkness is to amplify distraction. Maybe it's happening in your life this very moment and you don't even realize it. Distraction is very sneaky like that. The fix to all of this is as simple as it is hard. The way to beat distraction is to become captivated by something much bigger and much better, such as purpose and joy.

That's where we're headed in the pages of this book, and I want us to head that way for the rest of our lives. If you are willing to do the heavy lifting required, I promise you will trade up for something way better than what you've settled for so far. You will be replacing the distraction that robs your joy with the kind of purpose that nothing can ever take away.

Eyes forward. Buckle up. Here we go.

CHAPTER 2

THE KEYHOLE OF ETERNITY

Take care of your heart and grow your mind,
and you will live a life loaded with legacy.

I was sitting on the doctor's examination table . . . again. My whole life I have been a pretty healthy guy. Rick would be in soon to see what was going on with my heart rate. He has been our family doctor for decades, and I have literally trusted him with my life more than once. He has sewn up deep cuts and repaired a partially severed finger on one of my kids. He was by my side a few years ago when we figured out I caught an aggressive form of malaria while traveling in Africa. On that occasion, it was even money I'd be looking down from heaven by the end of the week, but Rick helped me through that one too.

He came in and we cycled through the standard pleasantries between a patient and a primary care physician, swapping stories like buddies do. Then Rick put the stethoscope on my chest. He must have just gotten it from the freezer or something. I took a startled breath as he leaned in and listened to my heartbeat. He asked about some of the symptoms I had been feeling, such as dizziness as soon as I stood up and shortness of breath just from going up the stairs. I mean, I am willing to confess I'm not the paragon of health, but I didn't think these symptoms were normal for the shape I was in.

Rick usually has a good poker face, but not this time. I watched as he furrowed his brow and focused his attention even more on my heartbeat. The concern I saw was unmistakable. In a hurry he brought a bunch of equipment into the room, put patches and cables on my chest, and started making recordings. The tape coming out of the machine had squiggles on it like a seismograph. Had this been a lie detector machine in disguise, he would've had enough wires attached to really get the goods on me.

After Rick was done with his bevy of tests, he looked me square in the face and said my heart wasn't beating the way it should. He rattled off some of the likely causes, and at the top of the list was that serious case of malaria. I won't go into details because I didn't fully understand all Rick said, but I knew it wasn't good news. In summary, my heart beat faster when I was sitting than some people's when they were running a marathon. It also didn't beat consistently.

Think of it this way: Your resting heart probably beats between 60 and 100 beats per minute if you're in average shape. Maybe a little slower if you're ripped and a little faster if you're not. Rather than the predictable *thump, thump, thump,* Rick recorded my heart beating rapidly and sporadically. It beat as fast as 220 beats per minute. It didn't take a medical degree to understand what could go wrong there. There's a big, long name for this condition, but the bottom line was, it didn't look like I would be breaking any records for "World's Oldest Living Person."

But I'm going to try anyway. Truth be known, I like the ring of 150 years old, which is the current age I'm aiming for. If I come up a little short, find a way to bury me on Tom Sawyer Island at Disneyland, okay? Even if you need to sneak me through the gate in a jar. I have a season ticket, so they won't mind.

Over the next several days, Rick got me appointments with some really smart cardiac specialists to confirm his findings and drill down on the core issues. After more freezing stethoscopes, wires, beeps, and furrowed brows, these experts said the only way to get my heart beating correctly again was to stop it momentarily and restart it with a huge electric jolt. You read that right. They would have to *stop my freaking heart* to help it find a new beat.

Here's my question for you: Would you do it? Would you be willing to risk dying in order for your life to be more lasting? Would you risk everything for the chance to live your life more fully? That's the kind of reset Jesus said following Him would entail. He told His friends it would be like dying and starting all over again. He said it would take something as drastic, invasive, and complete as a do-over to be fully His—undistracted by everything else.

We can all be new creations if we want to be. The cold hard truth is most people don't. We settle for the safe and distracted life we know rather than the one God has promised is available to us. Sure, we can agree that Jesus wants us to be new creations, but if we keep doing what we've always done, we've got to admit there's nothing new about it. A total reset isn't easy, and it involves risk. Maybe an enormous tragedy or loss causes us to reset. Or a reset might be the result of making time to clear our minds in the morning. Find a new rhythm for your heart. Here is my simple suggestion: Decide in advance that you will do whatever it takes to get your heart right, and then do it—even if it will kill all previous versions of you.

You need to ask yourself what makes your heart beat in ways that make you stronger, more courageous, more giving, and more loving. Figure out what makes your heart skip a beat with joy and what makes it miss a beat with dysfunction and distraction. Be willing to change all of it if you need to. Our hearts all beat a little differently, and I'm glad they do. Some thump fast, and others thump slow. Things that instantly blow your hair back might be a yawn for someone else. What totally bores you could totally light up someone else. What makes you weep may not cause someone else to notice. Something that is no big deal to you could fillet another to the bone. Be patient with each other when this happens. We all have a heart condition; it just shows itself in different ways. Someone who doesn't know me might make assumptions about my heart without knowing what it's actually doing. In the end, we're all looking through a keyhole at eternity as we try to figure out our lives today. Don't be distracted by how different you are from everyone else. Our hearts were meant to beat *together*, not the *same*.

If you want to dazzle heaven, stop being distracted being everyone else. Go be you. Do anything less, and the unique gift God wrapped in you will never be fully opened. Jesus said a rich relationship with the Father is only possible by having a right relationship with each other. In other words, if we say we love God but don't love the people He made, even the ones as weird and insecure and fallible as you and me, we have a heart condition we need to address. Don't keep ignoring, medicating, or being indifferent to it. If you want to find a richer faith than the one you have right now, the fix isn't more knowledge or arguments or distractions. Go be "one" with the people around you. You don't need to get in their faces to be in their lives. And don't just pursue the easy people either. If you want to move up to the graduate level class in this, find the difficult people around you and be "one" with them too. If you are thinking *yikes* about this new way of doing things, I'm right there with you, but it's a new heartbeat I want, not more of the failing one I've ended up with. Getting to a better place will require a restart.

Jesus' friends were distracted arguing about who got the big chairs next to Him in heaven. Jesus interrupted their silly argument by dropping some eternal clarity on them. He said that unless they changed and became like children, they would never enter the kingdom of God. I had been raised to think you just prayed a prayer and somehow the right combination of secret words opened up heaven's gates, but evidently there's more to it. It's a childlike faith—not a childish one—Jesus said would do the trick.

I showed up at the hospital to reset my heart. They gave me the dreaded blue hospital gown and escorted me to a room to prep me for the procedure. (By the way, can anyone explain to me why they need your entire backside exposed for this sort of thing when everything is happening on the frontside?) It was a little drafty, and I was trying to strategize how to avoid mooning everyone who walked by. Just then, a guy with a white coat came in and said he was the person who would be stopping and restarting my heart. That's all the information I had. Think about it for a second. For all I knew, the guy could have been a painter from Sherwin-Williams who found a stethoscope on the floor and threw it around his neck. Yet I trusted him to stop my heart and restart it. This all begs the question: What amount of additional information do you need before you will trust God to fix your heart?

The doctor and his team had me climb onto the gurney and lie down on my back. They hooked me to all kinds of monitors to make sure they didn't kill me too much—only just a little—when they stopped then restarted my heart. When Dr. Sherwin-Williams (I know his name and he's an amazing guy) started checking out the shock paddles, I gotta tell you, I was a mix of absolutely terrified and giddily excited. First, I had never done something like this, and I'm a junkie for new experiences. Second, I figured it would become a pretty boss story if I lived to tell about it. Third, if it actually worked, it would be like getting a new heart but without all the blood and scalpels and surgery for a transplant. Sure, like much of our lives, there was some amount of risk involved—but the benefits of a restart felt like a pretty good deal to me.

The doctor's assistants knocked me out with some kind of intravenous medicine, and I drifted off into a blur and then to nothingness. Before I went under, I imagined the man in the white coat rubbing a couple of paddles together, flipping on the defibrillator, and looking like Doc Brown from *Back to the Future* with a crazed look in his eyes as the machine emitted a steady, high-pitched hum. By the way, here's a fun little fact if you ever have to do this. Before they shock you, they make you take off any rings or metal jewelry because the voltage is enough to burn your skin under the metal. Also, pro tip: A weird number of my chest hairs got burned off. It's like a really violent waxing in this way.

And then I was awake! I felt like Scrooge on Christmas morning—a man with a new lease on life. I was hoping to see some Muppets singing carols to me when I opened my eyes, but instead the medical team hovered above me, checking all the monitors for my stability. When it was apparent I was in the clear, the doctor looked at me with a grin and said, "This isn't the afterlife; it worked." I was glad to hear this because I would've been disappointed to find heaven looking like a hospital room with bills and a copay. I also had banked heavily on my eternal heavenly garments having a backside. I suddenly had the heartbeat of a thirteen-year-old junior high school boy. And I still do.

In an average lifetime, we each get about 2.5 billion heartbeats. It takes a pretty strong muscle to beat this many times to send blood and oxygen from your toes to your ears. If you have ever squeezed a tennis ball, that's about how much effort one pump takes to give us life. What I'm saying is: It's not easy to be your heart, so take care of it, okay? Do this with your faith and also your relationships. Take care of them. Keep track of the stress you have subjected yourself to, and for Pete's sake, take care of your one amazing and irreplaceable body. We want to keep you around for a while.

My heart has a new rhythm now. It beats slow and strong. What about yours? Is your heart racing as you strive for things that won't last? Are you constantly distracted by the unimportant? Are you living in fear? After this procedure, the doctor said the best thing I could do for my heart is to not stress it out. Maybe that's good advice for you too. Our hearts are all different, but they can beat together even if they beat differently. Do whatever it takes to get there, even if it's a bit of a shock.

For the last several years, I've been telling myself that I want to be the guy who's available. That's why I put my cell phone number in the back of more than a million of my books. From the outside looking in, that probably looks like a move that would wreck any kind of productivity in my life. That's true, I suppose, if you're only trying to live an efficient, productive life. But I'm not, and here's why. We will be known for our opinions but remembered for the love we gave to everyone around us. If I have my head down over a project and can't be bothered to shift focus, I'll miss a good chance to show love and grace to the person next to me—and that's not the life I want to live. Receiving a truly ridiculous number of telephone calls each day is a great reminder of who I want to be. These don't feel like interruptions; they are reminders. What are you doing to remind yourself of who you want to be?

This availability has taken a fun new turn in the last couple of years. I started coaching some amazing people to help them navigate big things they want to accomplish for themselves, their families, their careers, and their faith. I have calls all week long with these new friends. Sure, it blows up my schedule pretty much every day to have these meetups on the calendar, but it also helps me fulfill my dream of being unreasonably available. That's my jam; it's my one solo hit; it's the etching on my life and will probably be on my headstone too. "Here lies Bob Goff; he was always available (but not now)." What do you want to be on yours? "Here lies [insert your name] who lived a distracted life"? If this has a ring of truth to it for you, the good news is that you have the power to change the epitaph.

One of the most important things I do after these coaching calls is to take notes on the conversation. At the end of each call I spend a solid five minutes reflecting on what we said and filling in the missing pieces I hadn't jotted down. Why? Because if I don't, a distraction is almost certain to wipe out any gains I've made. The ways we all process the conversations we have can become windows into our own important purposes. Writing notes is a great way to avoid distractions, not just because they help us remember things that resonated with us but also because they help us curate our points of view.

Take notes while you read this or any other book. Write down how you are going to apply the parts that make sense to you. If you don't net those butterflies immediately, I promise they will fly away. Do this, then study and refine those notes, and you will find connections between the ideas you have scribbled down in the middle of the conversation and ones you had in other conversations. You will capture meaningful, partially developed, and applicable ideas you can incorporate into your life. As you use what you have written down, they will create a feedback loop as they evolve into fuller, more complete ideas. If you don't take the time to capture and process your interior world, you will miss the opportunity to discover something bigger and more beautiful in your heart.

Many of the people who have brought a great deal of understanding and beauty to the world were notetakers. Marcus Aurelius, Beethoven, Lewis and Clark, Mark Twain . . . You name a person who was a standout in history, art, literature, or culture, and I bet you've just identified a notetaker. Benjamin Franklin wasn't a particularly virtuous guy, but he tracked a list of thirteen virtues, including notes on how he lived them out every day. You may not want to keep score of your character, but I am certain you will benefit from keeping track of it.

George Lucas, the famous moviemaker, wrote the script for *Star Wars* while also scoring *American Graffiti*. In those days of the industry, the way to locate a scene was to reference the roll of film it was on and the dialogue number within that roll of film. Someone asked George Lucas about a scene in *American Graffiti* that was on roll two, dialogue two. George wrote down in his notes "R2D2." I kid you not. He was spinning the puzzle piece in his mind for a lovable droid, took what would have been a completely unrelated written note, and . . . the rest is history. His note-taking became a way of harnessing and curating his creativity. It can do the same for you too.

Paul wrote a letter to his friends at a place called Corinth. He said that to him, their lives were just like letters from God to the world. He said they weren't a bunch of words carved into stone, but they were written on his and other people's hearts.[1] If you'll do the work, taking note of ideas and truths and thoughts that matter to you, you will put yourself in places to impact people in deep and inexplicable ways you couldn't have imagined. If you think of your life as a book that's being written, start taking better notes. It will become a masterpiece one sentence at a time.

Socrates said an unexamined life isn't worth living. I don't agree that such a life is not worth living, but I would concede we are prone to forgetting about self-reflection. If you have young kids or a stressful job, you especially know how hard life can be. Some days you crash into bed exhausted, just to get up and do it again . . . and again . . . and again. String together enough days like that, and you'll look up someday wondering where the years have gone. Don't get sucked into that trap. Write down all of the lessons you learned from each day. A life without reflection is like a vapor.

James, the brother of Jesus, said in one of his letters that none of us knows what will happen tomorrow. He said our lives are like a mist that appears for a little while and then vanishes.[2] I have seen this happen, and you have too. My favorite time to write and reflect is in the early morning. The dew is on the grass, and often there's a hint of fog in the air that collected overnight. Then each morning the dew melts away, the fog lifts, and the day begins. Taking good notes is a life hack for keeping your experiences and potential revelations from evaporating before your very eyes. The trick is to write down what you learn on the adventure so it doesn't go missing later.

There are twenty-five hundred creatures on earth known as "one-day insects." By contrast, one of the longest-living animals on earth is a type of deep-sea sponge that could be more than eleven thousand years old. If we lived that long, we would probably look like a bunch of sponges too. Most people are living like one-day insects, but we need to be a little more spongy by doing things that will last. I will say, though, don't throw shade at the one-day insects either. It'd be good to borrow some of their worldview because, like James said, we don't know what tomorrow will bring.

There is even one species of jellyfish that doesn't technically die at all. Get this: As soon as this kind of jellyfish gets really old, it reverts back to being a young jellyfish so it can grow up all over again. I want to be that kind of person, but holding on to the wisdom I've collected while returning to a childlike faith. Kind of like Benjamin Button, except I don't want to start out really old and get young; I want to start really young and grow wise. I want to pair the wisdom I gather over time with a greater accumulation of a childlike faith. How about you? If you're on board with this kind of life approach, what could you do to find your way back to a more innocent, engaged, and less distracted version of yourself?

Here's a truth you can take to the bank no matter how long you live: The clarity of purpose, undistracted energy, selfless love, and unselfish pursuits you bring to the world will be your legacy. Everything else will look like a distraction by comparison.

CHAPTER 3

BREAKING FREE BY COMING HOME

The cure for insecurity is being completely present in the expression of your purpose.

I've been trying to go to prisons more often—not as an inmate but as a friend. It wasn't my idea; it's something Jesus said we should do. From the outside, no jail is an inviting place. Anytime I pass by a prison, I get intimidated by the high barbed wire, razor wire, and windowless buildings. Some prisons even have guard towers and men carrying serious firepower as they monitor the perimeter. Going to places that are designed to keep people in doesn't feel natural, but that's exactly why I was compelled to start going. I think God asks us to give our presence, grace, and compassion to prisoners because He wants us to remember exactly how He saw us from the outside without the freedom Jesus promised.

The prison I visit most often is called San Quentin. It's actually an infamous place, though I'm not sure why a place of punishment should be famous. It was opened more than 160 years ago and has housed notorious prisoners, including Charles Manson. The prisoners have called it "The Arena" for almost a hundred years. It houses all the California inmates on death row, and in 1938 a gas chamber was installed that remained in use until 1996. There are no two ways about it: The place is rough but I have also developed friendships with the prisoners and courageous staff who have taught me a lot and have made me a better person.

I have taught a class there for some time with about 150 guys in it. They come from every walk of life. Some were brilliant businessmen who made big mistakes. Others killed someone, and a few didn't pay their taxes. They have one thing in common. They are all behind a large, guarded wall and will be for quite a long time. One day I got a call on my phone from one of the guys in my class named Kevin.

"Bob, I'm on the other side of the wall," he said.

Buddy, tell me there aren't a bunch of bedsheets tied together, hanging from a window, I was thinking.

"I'm out. They just released me!" he said excitedly through the phone he had borrowed.

Thinking this would be one of those Leonardo DiCaprio moments and anticipating an answer that would change my life, I asked, "Buddy, what was your first thought when you stepped outside?"

Kevin paused and then said, "I realized . . . I've got pockets!"

Wait, what? It was hardly the big, deep, theological thing I was expecting him to say. But the more I thought about it, I realized it was a big, deep, theological thing he had said.

"Be really careful what you put in them, Kevin," I said in a moment of clarity.

We all have pockets. It's what we put in them or keep in them that can become distractions. Regrets, resentment, hurts, and misunderstandings are all things that can become huge distractions.

———

I was walking in the prison yard with a few of the guys from class. Men were lifting weights the size of a Prius with the effort it takes me to move a stapler. I joked to the guy standing next to me that if I had a barbell with weights on it, I could imagine the bar alone crushing my chest until a couple of guys lifted it off.

Later that day in class we were sitting in a circle. I told the guys about my conversation in the yard and asked if there was anything they needed to get off their chests. We went around the circle and the guy sitting to my left talked about the difficult time he was having with his cellmate, which wasn't surprising given the size of their cell—four-and-a-half-feet wide and ten feet, eight inches long, housing two guys each weighing 250 pounds or more. The guy next to him told us he was feeling estranged from the family he had been separated from for more than a decade. His wife was planning on moving on, and he was really sad. I could only imagine how difficult and hopeless it would feel for both of them.

We went around the circle, and eventually the guy sitting next to me on my right was up. He looked at the floor for a long time, then lifted his head and looked each of the guys in the eyes. "I've been here for eighteen years and I've been telling everybody I didn't do it." He paused, took a deep breath, and said, "I did it." Around the circle he didn't see judgment; he saw acceptance. In that moment he was the freest guy I had ever met. This is what honesty and vulnerability will do every day if we'll let it.

Shame keeps us behind the walls we have constructed to keep

everybody out. So do envy and bitterness and judgmental people. Most of pride's prisoners think they are the guards. What we need is the kind of jailbreak an accepting community can offer. Find one and experience the kind of freedom and focus you didn't think was possible for you.

A little closer to home in San Diego I was visiting a young man in his early twenties in our local jail. He had made some stupid mistakes that had cost him his freedom. He was scared, lonely, and needed some company. I was a family friend and thought he would enjoy some time together. I had done visits like this before and knew we would meet in a room that felt a lot like a jail cell, designed for lawyers and clients to meet and discuss their cases. For me, it was just a place I could meet with a scared kid. This room is encased in a thicker-than-normal layer of concrete, with bulletproof glass, a heavy door, and several electronic locks.

The guards locked us in. Ironically, those who visit prisoners become prisoners themselves. There's always a sense of heaviness and depression in these rooms, as if they are designed to eliminate any sense of warmth or hope or humanity. The whole space screams, "Don't even think about it!"

My young friend was escorted into the room. His handcuffs were removed, and we exchanged a few words as we settled into our chairs. I tried my best to exude signals of grace and empathy and acceptance as he told his story. Then something happened—like the moment in a movie where everything goes horribly wrong. The entire jail lost electricity. The whole thing. The overhead lights in our room clicked off, and emergency floodlights clicked on. The room went into complete lockdown triggered by the loss of power, and not even the guards could get in. Had the walls not been so thick, I probably would have heard the generator powering up to make sure the entire complex didn't devolve into complete pandemonium. What if there were guys in the yard sniffing out their opportunity to escape? What if a group was in the mess hall and a huge fight broke out? Did I mention this was a jail housing lots of inmates? When something like this happens, things can go sideways fast.

For the next four hours, I was stuck in this room with the young man. I tried making a call, but there was no cell service. I couldn't receive any calls for the same reason. I wanted out, big-time. If I had a rock hammer, I would have dug a hole and crawled through a sewer pipe to get out.

Nothing much happened despite the Hollywood setup. My new friend was still just as scared and in need of a friend after four hours. I needed a new pair of underwear, but I got over the experience eventually. It dawned on me that a room designed for maximum security had become a place of total insecurity. And that got me thinking about the role insecurity has played in my life and in my friends' lives. We expend so much energy trying to feel secure and hide any sense we are afraid. We construct walls and put up our bulletproof glass so nothing can hurt us. Sadly, we can spend our entire lives constructing a façade of security and safety, when inside we are just scared people in need of a friend.

Do you need the courage to admit, even now, that you have been pretending to be something you are not? Are you a prisoner needing space to get real? Have you been distracted by your need to never seem weak or afraid or vulnerable? Are you spending weird amounts of time trying to control the people around you because your life on the inside is out of control? How much energy is that taking out of you—energy you could pour into something bigger and more beautiful than your insecurities?

We're all inwardly insecure to some degree. What shrouds this from view is that each of us deals with our insecurities differently and, as a result, only some of us look outwardly insecure. Some people can speak in public while others can't. Some people are afraid of spiders, and others collect tarantulas. Some people get quiet as a church mouse when they are insecure, and others get mean as a rattlesnake. If you want to dazzle God, don't ignore, dismiss, or deny your insecurities, and don't overlook other people's odd behaviors as the groans of insecurities make their way to the surface. Understand and embrace these things instead. Don't let them take you prisoner. Figure out where they came from and send them back there. Master these feelings when they're blocking your way forward, and choose to live undistracted by them. We are not the average of the five most insecure people who have opinions about us; we're the product of the several most focused and undistracted people we successfully imitate.

None of this is easy because we all live incredibly conflicted lives. It just comes with the package of being human. Paul, a writer of many of the letters in the Bible, said he was frustrated that he kept doing the things he didn't want to do and didn't do the things he longed to do.[1] I can relate to that, and I bet you can too. The reason is simple. Life is full of push; life is full of pull. What I mean is, we are pushed by our insecurities and pulled by anything we think will help us avoid looking as insecure as we actually are. We're fickle creatures, and sometimes it's hard to know if we're coming or going.

So how do we connect who we are with who we want to be when each force is tugging us in a different direction? We're not unlike Peter Pan, who got separated from his shadow. You remember the scene. Peter is bouncing around the room chasing his shadow, which is no longer attached to him. This is where most of us live—detached, distracted, and frantic but trying to look like we're not. After Peter chases his shadow around the room as it bounces off of the walls and ceiling, he eventually catches up to it. Peter doesn't need a bunch of information in this moment; he needs a friend to help him get reconnected with his shadowself. Peter wants to use soap to reattach his shadow, but thankfully Wendy breaks out a needle and thread for a more permanent fix. People who live with purpose are willing to be sewn back together; they're willing to admit they're separated in the first place, and they're willing to have some safe friends get involved to help put them back together.

Come home to yourself. Get reacquainted with your true self, which is the you everyone sees plus the shadow they don't. Give yourself a pep talk about how it's okay to be exactly who you are. The people I enjoy the most aren't looking to me for validation; they have already arrived there for themselves knowing they are not perfect but that God loves them anyway. They recognize that life is trying to put them in a prison cell of head fakes and faulty expectations. It's refreshing to be around them, and if this is the kind of person you are becoming, lay out the red carpet and invite these people into your life. Decide to ditch insecurity and replace it with God's brand of acceptance. Try it. Nothing feels quite so good as tossing off toxic expectations and the distractions of unhealthy peers, workmates, family, and the world around you as you settle into the joy of simply being you.

When I became a grandfather, I decided to stay a whole lot closer to home. If you have read any of my other books, you probably know I quit things on Thursdays. On a Thursday in early January a few years back, I canceled seventy-two speaking events in one day. It was a costly decision, but I didn't want to miss a moment with my grandkids. My whole life had been building for this new era.

Most people were gracious and accepting of my decision, but one event in Arizona said they would be in a tight spot if I didn't come. They asked me to reconsider, and they were really gracious about it. I didn't want to leave them in a crack, so I decided I would go. A crowded commercial flight felt a little dicey at the time because of what was unfolding in the world, and since I have a pilot's license, I decided to rent a cheap private airplane and fly it myself. It seemed like a great work-around at the time.

The daytime flight from San Diego to Arizona was uneventful, and after the gathering wrapped up, it was time to fly home. It was late at night, and I needed to cross back over the desert and mountain range that separates San Diego from Phoenix. I took off into the night sky, with a dark desert below and ebony skies above. My view was completely black except for the flight instruments in my cockpit. There is a quiet beauty in those moments, and I welcomed the trip back.

Flying over uninhabited places like this is a little trickier than flying over a city because there are no lights below and no lights on the horizon. It's kind of like being inside a canvas sack or a subterranean cave where you can't see your hand waving in front of your face. As a result, it's easy to get disoriented, and you need to rely on the instruments so you don't end up flying in circles or accidentally find yourself descending and hitting something. That's why I was more than a little anxious when two of the instruments on the rented plane went offline over the desert. One moment they were working, and the next they simply weren't. I snapped to attention as if I had just chugged a case of Red Bull.

Things got really tense really fast. Here's what I did: I leveled the wings and climbed a little higher to make sure I flew over the tops of the mountains ahead. I did this for the next couple of hours, and eventually the glow of the San Diego city lights came into view.

I was reminded how good it feels when we return home. Here's my point: Don't let the darkness of your circumstances or the surprises you encounter distract you from your destination. Level the wings, climb a little higher, look for the glow of home, then aim for it.

I'm an optimist by nature. If I heard the sky was falling, I'd get a net to catch some. You never know when a little blue sky will come in handy, right? The cynics from biblical times weren't anything like modern-day ones. Far from it. The old-school cynics lived simple and unassuming lives. One of their pioneers, Diogenes, lived in a large ceramic water jar. Not unlike your first apartment, I bet. He spent the days walking through Athens carrying a lit lantern. When asked why he did this in the daylight hours, he said he was looking for men and women who were living virtuous lives. Find these people today and surround yourself with them. Look for virtues, not flaws, in the people around you, and you will find a beautiful path forward in your life.

Modern-day cynics don't roll this way. It seems like they always wake up on the wrong side of the bed. They are like snipers, but they are far from courageous. They elevate themselves, then camouflage their positions. They hide in the lofty places they construct, then take potshots at the people they want to exert control over. If you don't agree with them or don't yield to their opinions, you become a target yourself. I wouldn't have wanted to have a cynic as a copilot during my nighttime flight, and you shouldn't have one in your life either. If you play the cynic, please stop, for your sake and ours. I know you think you are being helpful, but the hard truth is, you are not. You may not realize it, but you are a distraction.

I don't think this is an overstatement: Modern-day cynicism has likely cost the world hearts, lives, cures for diseases, and trillions of dollars. It has also ruined plenty of holiday dinners. Don't be the cynic in your circles. You will only be dragging people down and distracting them with your doom and gloom. Recognize that cynics simply wear their insecurities on their sleeves and subconsciously try to create a low common denominator. Modern-day cynics would probably just say they're realists, but I'm not buying it.

You are not without a remedy if you are on the receiving end of a boatload of negative vibe. Every time a cynic hands you a dark invitation to join them on their journey, just hand it right back to them. They're offering you a ride in a car with no tires that has been riding on the rims for years. That's why they make so much noise and are surrounded by sparks. Take the bus. Walk if you must. Just don't hitch a ride with cynics anymore. It's a one-way trip to a life filled with distractions.

Besides, I've never met a courageous cynic. Have you? I *have* encountered a lot of distracted ones who are trying to convince other people to join them. Don't take the bait. Even in our faith communities, where you would expect to find a place of abundant love and acceptance, you will find people who gather to gossip and try to control the behaviors of people they disagree with by pointing bony fingers and lobbing sharp words in their direction. Don't get distracted by this mutation of faith. You'll know you have found the right community when all the talk is about Jesus and what He did with His life—not someone's opinions about what you ought to be doing with yours.

———

This is a safe space we're in together, so let me ask you a few questions. What are you doing with your life? Have you drifted from a place that feels like home? Have you demoted yourself from an optimist looking for virtue to a modern cynic? Are you quick to anger and dismay, or do you find silver linings and possibilities everywhere you look? What would it take to begin looking for the virtues in people and the circumstances you find yourself in?

These are deep and serious questions, and I hope you answer them in your own heart with honesty, acceptance, and grace . . . even if you don't like the answers. If you're going to live an undistracted life of immense purpose, it must begin with brutal honesty. If you haven't tried that yet, let me tell you a surprising secret. It is refreshing and freeing to tell yourself the truth. Don't be afraid to call it what it is. Have you gotten sidetracked by these distractions of the soul? I know I have from time to time. Most of us have. God did not design your life to be a prison. He broke the shackles and knocked down the doors already. Don't let a lie hold you back any longer. You are as free as you are willing to allow yourself to be. God invites all of us to step out into the sunlight. He's waving us toward the plane.

I know it is sometimes dark, but level the wings, get some altitude, keep your eye on the compass, and point your life toward Jesus.

CHAPTER 4

THE HAPPINESS OF PURSUIT

*Distraction can capture your calendar
and hijack your happiness.*

When I was learning to fly, I realized early on there is an acronym for almost everything in aviation. For instance, before you take off or land, you do a GUMPS check. That means you make sure the *gas* is set to the tank with the most fuel in it so you don't run out near the ground. You next check the *undercarriage* of the airplane to make sure the wheels are down and locked—always a good call. In order to have the power to take off or go around and try again if the landing doesn't go as planned, you need to have the fuel *mixture* as rich as possible. The controls for the *propeller* on an airplane can change the pitch at which it cuts through the air and need to be set for maximum power as well. Finally, *seat belts* need to be fastened and checked.

You will hear a few stories each year about someone who ran out of gas and crashed, came in on the belly of the plane because they forgot to lower the wheels, or didn't have the power they needed to lift off. You would think these things would be obvious to anyone with a license to fly, but with all the decisions a pilot must make in a short period of time, even the most experienced commercial pilots risk missing important steps. So they do a GUMPS check before every takeoff or landing to organize the flow of the decisions.

The trick in aviation is to have a quiet cockpit. By that, I mean you need to avoid getting distracted by what is going on outside the cockpit and losing track of what is going on inside. Tragically, this is what happened to basketball legend Kobe Bryant, his daughter, and seven others on board. The pilot became disoriented by what was happening outside of the cockpit, resulting in a devastating crash. Quiet down your life if it has become loud. Find a couple of safe friends and bring all the activity in your life down a notch or two.

How many decisions would you guess you make in a typical day? A dozen? One hundred? Does one thousand sound a little closer? Get this. Each of us makes about thirty-five thousand decisions every day. More if you spend an hour in a candy store. Some decisions are mundane, and some are major. We decide where we will live, if we will marry and who we will marry, the job we will accept and the one we will quit. The car we will buy or the bus we will take. The cake or veggies we will eat. (Go with the cake for the win.) Who we will believe and who we won't, where we will go and how long we will stay, the faith we will embrace or ignore, and countless other decisions.

Here's a surprising thing though: Most of us never decide to be happy. I bet most of us think "happy" is a result of other choices, but that's not all of it. Sure, circumstances can be truly awful, but feeling happy is a choice just like any other. It's not that we don't want to be happy; we just get distracted by so many unhappy things that we never get back around to happiness. Perhaps we think we need an invitation or permission to be happy. And what if we want happy feelings to transition into a deep and abiding joy with a longer shelf life?

Consider this. In stark contrast to our complicated decision tree, a child makes less than 10 percent of the decisions adults make each day. Maybe one of the benefits of the childlike faith Jesus said we need is that there are fewer decisions to make, and hence, fewer distractions to manage. Have you seen a kid with a pile of Legos? It's like the rest of the world doesn't even exist. They are lost in the beautiful singularity of creative joy and purpose they find in their play. They don't care if they are early or late for the next thing. They are fully present and completely undistracted. All the while, heaven dances and celebrates the simple beauty of a child at play and invites us to do the same. Perhaps we should take a lesson or two from the children around us: get fully engrossed in something lasting we care about, eliminate some of the decisions we make, and find our joy again.

Most people hope they'll find happiness at home, but the hard truth is, they aren't around long enough to experience what's already waiting for them there. Simple and complicated distractions take us away from the people we love. When this occurs, the result is both subtle and toxic. We start to settle for proximity rather than presence with each other. Know what I mean? You will know this is happening to you if you only listen for the highlights in your loved one's conversations without taking note of the emotions and body language that are also present in the room. These distractions are masked in familiar disguises like career, appointments, and promotions. They invade our homes and come dressed as extracurricular activities, sports, and electronic screens. They look like business calls and video games and Zoom conferences and television shows and committees and meetings and sometimes even churches.

If we want to live more undistracted lives, we need to get real and admit that busyness is actually hijacking our joy. Here's the good news: We can fix all this just as easily as we messed it up. Get a couple of baseball gloves and talk to your loved ones about your day as you throw the ball around. If you answer your cell phone while playing catch, you'll lose teeth. This is what it looks like to really get some skin in the game. Get some wood and light a fire. Find some chairs and fill them with people you haven't connected with in a while, then watch the flames dance. Go ahead and get some smoke on you, and the next day your clothes will smell like a dozen great conversations.

Do this with some urgency too. You don't have as much time as you think you have. Take it from a guy who's been around for a while. There's a saying that I have found to be generally true: The days are long, but the years are short. If you fill your days with trivial stuff, you will look up one day and a year or a decade or a half-century will have passed. Don't wait until you are old to ask yourself: *What have I done with all that time?* Why not ask yourself right now? *What am I going to do with all the time ahead of me?* What do you want your answer to be? Once you decide what you want the future to look like, make a couple of moves like your life is actually yours to live—because it is. Quit the job, call the friend, make the apology, launch the dream, take the shot . . . heaven is just hoping we will.

I've spent some time exploring the branches on my family tree, and it turns out that most Goff men come from the factory like a windup toy with only a certain number of turns. We're Energizer bunnies who just stop pounding our drums and tip over at about the same age. Because we all seem to keel over at about the same time, I've bracketed those dates for myself and have a clock that counts down from then to remind me how many days I have left. Does this sound crazy or morbid? I don't think it's either; I think it's brilliant. Try it. Figure out how much longer you think you'll live, set a timer to countdown from there, and see how it changes your days. I bet you'll have fewer arguments and scroll social media less. You will look for more rainbows, find more waterfalls, and watch more sunsets. You'll surf the waves instead of surfing the web, and you'll trade reality shows for . . . actual reality. Simply put, your real life will be so good that none of the artificial stuff will distract you anymore.

It's easy to fall into the "I'll be happy *when* . . ." trap. We tend to think that happiness is something *out there* that we need to attain. This kind of deferral feels safe, but listen closely: It isn't. Instead, what if you begin declaring for yourself with God's help "I *will* look for joy" without any qualifiers or add-ons? Paul talked about something on a deeper level. He talked about being content.[1] Why not go all-pro with this? Substitute the word *content* or the words *fully present* for the word *happy*, and you'll really have a ball game: "I *will* be content." "I *will* be fully present." These declarations can create tremendous untapped power in your life. Here is the astounding part. You hold all the levers to make this happen if you want to. Does this mean you can control all your circumstances, setbacks, outcomes, and disappointments? Of course not. You can, however, influence them. We can eliminate the distractions that have been obscuring our view of what God is doing in the world. We will be changed from the inside out.

We don't need to hedge our bets against disappointment by keeping our expectations low. This wide, deceptive, and potholed off-ramp isn't worth taking, and it won't get you anywhere worthwhile. Assume instead that God is going to do inexplicably, wildly, unfathomably more than you could have ever seen or imagined. If that doesn't make you feel a little happy and joyful, you need a sundae.

And again, before you're too quick to dismiss "being happy" or finding joy as a wasteful extravagance or cotton candy for the brain, let's think about it for a second. People who are happy and filled with joy get a ton more accomplished than people who aren't. It's true, and the only ones who can't see this are usually the unhappy ones.

If you choose happiness and joy, then kindness and empathy and engagement are the outcomes. If joy is going on inside of us, everyone will know because it will be expressed outwardly as kindness and caring and action in your life. You'll be nicer, and trust me when I say this is what the earth needs more of. Why am I telling you to be nice in a book about distraction? The primary reason is because people who aren't nice distract everyone around them. You know it's true, and if you are one of the not-nice people, you are in fact banking on this cause and effect. We are not going to get to the important, courageous, purposeful work of being the most priceless versions of ourselves if we aren't being nice to ourselves or the people around us. Don't confuse "nice" with fake or artificial. Find your joy, and you will find a reservoir of honor and respect and empathy and caring for others. In a word, you'll be nicer to be around.

But here is something you already know: It's hard to be nice all the time. Take me, for example. I think I'm a pretty nice guy. (I have asked around to confirm this.) Still, I'm not even close to being nice most of the time. I bet there are people who think I'm subtle about not being nice to the people around me. They see a tone, a gesture, a snarky word, subtle body language, or a roll of my eyes as signs of my disapproval. Often the people who have built a case about how not-nice you are lack quite a bit of niceness too. The truth is, we use up a crazy amount of energy sorting out other people's mean streaks or controlling ours—wasting energy that would be better spent living the big lives Jesus said are available to us.

I have a family member who is really difficult, or at least used to be. The last time I spoke to this person was at my wedding—almost thirty-five years ago. Let that sink in for a second. The guy who wrote books titled *Love Does* and *Everybody, Always* has this problem? Perhaps I should have named these books *Love Does (but Only Sometimes)* or *Everybody, Always (Except This Difficult Family Member)*. How about you? If you were punishingly honest, what would be the name of the book your life is writing?

Remember this: Most disagreeable people out there don't think they are mean. They think they are right. If you are a person of faith, at some point you'll need to decide whether you want to be right or if you want to be Jesus. Choose wisely, because you are picking more than just an argument; you are picking your legacy. If you're having a hard time being kind rather than grinding the gears, perhaps it would do you well to push in the clutch and figure out what's driving this behavior. We're not here to judge and evaluate other people's lives; we should be the ones who are cheering from the stands and waving our arms in the air in anticipation of what comes next in someone's life. When being right gets in the way of being kind, we need to catch our breath and decide who we want to be all over again.

Jerks are quickly forgotten, but one act of kindness laced with joy can be remembered forever. Besides, the world seems to be full of jerks these days—and if you're mean, it makes mean people look normal, and this shouldn't be the standard.

Distraction robs us of the ability to both live in the moment and discern what lasts. It can feel delicious to throw a jab at someone you disagree with or don't like, particularly if they are taking a ridiculous or untenable position. It can be reassuring for a short time to experience "us versus them" because it gives us a sense of belonging to a posse of equally enraged people. But our ultimate residence doesn't have a return address on earth, so looking for things that last is always a good long-term play.

When I was a Boy Scout, we spent an exorbitant amount of time learning how to build, tend, and properly extinguish campfires. The scoutmaster would walk us through the forest surrounding our campsite pointing out which wood was long-lasting and good to burn as well as other wood that would produce a big flame but only for a short time. In case it helps you next time you're camping, here's a tip: Hardwoods like oak are great to burn; softwoods like pine aren't. Oak burns nicely and with little smoke; pine flames up bright like a roman candle but soon is gone. He taught us that if you want a fire to burn long and hot, you have to choose the right wood. That'll preach. If you want to make a big impact in the world, stop throwing pine on the fire in your life and burn the oak instead. Play the long game. Paul told his friends no less. He reminded them to fan the flames of the fire God had lit in their lives.[2] In short, if you want the right kind of flame, get the right kind of wood.

If you want to start burning a little hotter in your life, don't keep giving in to the selfishness that creates distractions for you. It's like putting green wood on the fire. Here's why. We can't bring the heat if we're distracted trying to burn the green wood that is readily available. Shame is green wood. So are envy and comparison. Worries are green wood in your life. Unnecessary arguments are green wood too. All you'll get is smoke from these.

Lose the handheld distractions. Think of phone use as cheating on your family. If you have a habit of constantly checking your screens, don't be hard on yourself. Just find a better habit. Make pasta, raise hummingbirds, buy a drum set or a tuba. Get a gun safe and put your phone in it when you get home. Give your wife or your kids the key or the combination. Give yourself reminders about the importance of being fully present for your family and not missing anything. Change the ringtone on your cell phone to "Cat's in the Cradle" sung by Harry Chapin. You'll pick up the phone less and your kids more.

If you want to see change in your life, take a realistic look at where you are right now. How are you spending your time? Write down on a paper plate how much time you spend with your family. Think of the whole plate as a pie chart of the twenty-four hours you get each day. If you spend eight hours sleeping, terrific. Get nine if you need it. But shade in that part of the paper plate. How much time do you spend working, whether physically at the job site or not? Be honest. Don't shade in how little time you *wish* you spent working. Mark off the amount of time you actually spend in the different areas of your life. If the lines have become blurred to you, ask someone you love or live with for an estimate. You might be bummed by their answer, but let's get the truth out there. At least you will know what you are dealing with.

Ask yourself how much undistracted time you are spending with the ones you love. If you're married, how often are you going deeper and practicing authenticity? Shade it in. Don't forget the time you spend pursuing things that give you joy and purpose and encouragement—whether it's reading a book, riding a unicycle, or taking a peaceful walk in the park. People living with heaps of purpose and direction have an inversely proportional amount of distraction they allow into their lives. Take a good look at your plate when you have figured out what is happening in your life. You'll know you're distracted if the sizes of your pie pieces don't match the shape of the life you want.

Don't be discouraged if you don't like what you see. Here's the fix. Surround yourself with reminders of who you are and what you want. Set alarms marking the end of one activity and the beginning of full engagement in the next one. Make a family flag. Put images and symbols on it that will remind you of what matters most to your family. Raise that flag over your house and your life each day. A flag also helps you tell people what you need. If it's a chocolate cake, put that on a flag and run it up the flagpole. Our friends won't know what we need if we don't signal it to them.

Take steps back toward the friends and loved ones you have grown distant from. Chase after them like they've got something of yours, because they do. When something goes wrong, instead of saying to your friends, "I hope you feel better," figure out how to help them actually get better. This will require sacrifice and commitment on your part, but people who are no longer living distracted lives do things like this for the people they care about.

Don't you see? The clock is ticking. Your years can get sidelined by the many daily decisions life demands of you. Maybe you need to break out of some of the routines you have settled into. Remember, for many of us, distraction is the norm—the default position. When you overload your life with decisions that seem important but aren't, you forgo the chance to choose happiness and joy.

So, where do you start? Well, there are as many starting points as you have excuses. First, have the difficult talk with yourself you've been deferring. You might need to break up with your past. I know it will be awkward to make the needed changes, but make them anyway. Declare yourself completely free from those distractions and habits and activities that have become familiar but are no longer serving you. Make room for a couple of new routines that lead to who you are becoming, then replace all the earlier habits you had adopted that obscured the path.

Did you know the Declaration of Independence is only thirty-six sentences long? If a ragtag patchwork of colonies broke up with

England in thirty-six sentences, you can break up with your distractions in a dozen. Do you need a sentence about negative self-talk? Write it down. Put that nonsense on notice because you're quitting it entirely. Declare "it's not me, it's you. I'm out." What about shame or people-pleasing? Kick them to the curb. What about asking for permission to do the things you already have permission to do? You will only be as free as you actually believe you are. Write your "Declaration Against Distraction" and then buckle up. You have just created the space for an abundance of joy and purpose to come flooding into your life.

CHAPTER 5

HOW MANY FINGERS AM I HOLDING UP?

Be captivated with purpose and you'll care less about everyone's predictions.

When I was a kid, someone in my class started a rumor that I was a child prodigy. It didn't last long, but I had the title for at least a week. It wasn't me who started the rumor, but it would have been a great idea if I had been smart enough to think of it. Before that bubble burst, though, they transferred me to some highfalutin school for gifted kids. In one day I broke enough rules that they booted me right back out. I don't recall the offenses, but whatever they were, they must have been whoppers. Who knows—maybe I didn't understand the ninth value of pi or that *isosceles* was a triangle instead of an ice cream. I couldn't go back to my previous school, either, because of rules in the school district. So there I was, permanently kicked out of kindergarten. What I did must be under seal or something because I have never found out the offense. When I arrived home, I remember that my mom was up on a ladder painting the stucco behind the house. All she said was, "I'm so disappointed." She shook her head, and that was that. I don't know if either of us ever fully bounced back from this letdown. Thus, my illustrious career as an underperformer began.

My second run at kindergarten came a year later. I passed with flying colors. No, literally, they said I could throw crayons farther than anyone in class. It was then, even at a young age, that my parents started to realize my Legos didn't stack up the same way everyone else's did.

When I was in elementary school, things weren't like they are now. Back then, there were two types of classes for each grade: the class for the smart kids and the class for the dumb kids and the troublemakers. The people in charge of placement must have read my file because they put me straight in with the rest of the underperformers. I remember my teacher, Mr. Ramos. He was the only guy teacher at the school, and he was huge—like NFL linebacker huge. He was an intimidating figure to all of us eight-year-olds, with his bulky biceps, vein-popping forearms, and an annoyed stare that would make a puppy whimper. I guess the school thought this island of misfit toys needed a heavy hand to keep us in line because Mr. Ramos let us know early on that he wasn't going to take any "shenanigans" from us. I put that word in quotation marks because I distinctly remember him saying something much different and more threatening. He got the point across to us that he was the boss.

There was a guy named Mark in class. At age eight, he was almost as big as the teacher. He was the leader of our little group.

During recess, we concocted elaborate schemes about how to take Mr. Ramos down, and we met as a group to plan it out using Cheetos, milk cartons, and the sandwich crusts our moms forgot to cut off. We were clearly a pretty tough crowd. I didn't know Mark's background, but I figured he must be in the mafia or something. I wondered out loud on the playground if someone can be in the mafia when they're eight, and Mark confirmed that, indeed, one could.

I'm sad to say I didn't pull out of this low-grade mediocrity for a very long time. For many, many more years, in fact. All the while, my parents' disappointment in me compounded with every bad report card. When I finally reached high school, I still wasn't much of a student. The words *college material* weren't used with my name in the same sentence by any of the counselors at school. A diploma is all anyone expected of me, and I checked that box when I miraculously graduated. The trajectory for me seemed to be that I would do some workaday whatever until retirement age. Then I'd draw Social Security until the government wouldn't let me anymore or the system went broke. To the people I looked up to the most, I was always a few eggs shy of a dozen. I didn't have the wattage to live up to the expectations they put in place for me, and it didn't occur to me to find some different storyline to live by. It would take a little while longer for that to fully happen, but something small had already started to shift in my mind.

As a student, my goal was to complete the minimum requirements for a diploma, then aim for doing a little bit less. If I could hit that mark without being expelled or jailed, I figured, my time in high school would be a success. I sat through the odd English or math class, but I filled my schedule mostly with shop classes. Shop class was the only place high school made sense to me, so I signed up for every version of it: metal shop, auto shop, electrical shop, and wood shop. If "marching band shop" had been a thing, I would have signed up for it and carried an acetylene welder under my arm.

Mr. Hodgkins was the wood shop teacher. He was a terrific guy. He seemed ancient at the time, which meant he was more than thirty years old. He had a deep Southern accent that made him fun to listen to. He had no guile, an easy smile, and a disarming demeanor. He talked to every student like an equal and treated us as if we were smart enough to avoid shooting our feet with nail guns, slurping the wood glue, or sticking wooden dowels up our noses. You know how I know? The first day of class, he gave the same speech he had given every class every term: "Don't shoot yusselves with thuh nail gun or eat the wood glue or put dowels up your noses, okay?" We all nodded blankly. Everyone liked him a lot.

I remember a lot more about Mr. Hodgkins. He wore plaid shirts and lumberjack boots all the time, probably even to bed. He was gruff and kind. His face was a little wrinkled from the years, and he often walked down the hallways covered in wood shavings. The most distinctive thing about Mr. Hodgkins's appearance, though, was that he only had three fingers on his right hand. The others went missing somewhere along the way.

Whenever we had a new project, Mr. Hodgkins showed us how to use the tools in the shop that we would need. He gave a demonstration with some scrap pieces of wood and then invited us up to try. We learned how to use the sander and the drill press and the lathe. That semester I got so excited thinking about the big project I was going to build—a da Vinci–designed set of wings I could wear to fly a short distance. Just kidding, I ended up making a lamp, proving I could turn twenty dollars' worth of wood into a five-dollar item with an uncanny predictability.

Close to the end of class one day, it was time to use the biggest of all the shop tools: the table saw. Mr. Hodgkins ambled up to us and got real serious as we huddled around this large piece of equipment. I'm not sure why, but there was a nervous energy in the room, as if we were all about to cliff dive or something. We were scared and exhilarated at the same time. Mr. Hodgkins stood next to the saw and patted the table surface. Then his hand hovered over the slit where the blade would emerge, the empty spaces of his missing fingers making a ghostly caress where the sharp tines would soon rise up. "Now this one . . . y'all need to be *reeeal* careful with this one." We all stared at his missing fingers and tried not to stare at the same time.

Mr. Hodgkins moved his hand back, then flipped a switch, and the blade sprang to life out of sight under the table. The shop was filled with the high-pitched fury of metal teeth spinning hundreds of times per second. Mr. Hodgkins reached below the table and began spinning another wheel. As he did, the blade slowly rose into view and into a cutting position. For effect, Mr. Hodgkins turned around and looked at us with a mischievous smirk and raised eyebrows in between each step. He put a piece of wood on the table and slid it slowly toward the blade, which sliced it thin like toast. He pushed the wood slowly through the blade and yelled back at us, "You gotta let the blade do the work. Don't push too hard. You'll know how it feels after you do it a few times."

He continued to cut the wood, pushing with his hands until there wasn't enough wood to keep his fingers at a safe distance from the circular blade. Mr. Hodgkins stopped, turned off the table saw, and got everybody's attention. He had us step closer. "Now, make sure y'all don't get your fingers close to the blade, okay?" He was very intent when he said this as he locked into eye contact with every single one of us. "When the end of the wood gets to about right here, get a poosh stick and poosh it through." We all knew he meant "push," but it came out "poosh" with his accent. We all grinned.

Clearly Mr. Hodgkins had not used a poosh stick at some point. Do you think it made him less trustworthy because he made an epic mistake that cost him some digits? Of course not. We didn't trust him less because he had failed; we trusted him more. His failure had been an obvious one. The problem is that many of our failures are not, and we miss the opportunity to earn people's trust when we aren't courageous enough to get real and transparent about them.

I tried to imagine Mr. Hodgkins's fateful day and what it must have felt like for him. Maybe he was already a wood shop teacher, or maybe he was an aspiring one. I don't think you just stumble into teaching wood shop. So Mr. Hodgkins probably had a good bit of experience with things like table saws. Maybe he grew up around his dad or mom building things with wood and learned how to use the tools. It's a guess, but I wonder if he got distracted one day and lost some fingers. Still, he stuck with it. Here's what I wonder about—when you fail or have a setback, will you?

Just because Mr. Hodgkins failed to follow the poosh stick rule in the past didn't mean he was disqualified from giving us some pointers. In a way it made him *more* qualified because he was living proof of what the oversight could cost. I didn't see him as deficient; I saw him as a kind and capable guy with some real-life experience to back up his instruction.

Do you suppose Mr. Hodgkins had to wrestle with a sense of disappointment and shame from having made a mistake? Perhaps, but despite this, his love of teaching and working with wood propelled him forward, not backward. He learned some hard and no doubt painful lessons, but he turned these setbacks into something beautiful in our lives. That's what people living with purpose and joy decide to do.

Finding your life's purpose will entail some failure and more than a few pushbacks along the way. You know the expression:

"Resistance is key." An athlete needs it to build muscle, cars need it to travel, the space shuttle needs it to slow down, and you need it to grow. Don't be too quick to self-identify as the victim when you are the student. Resist compiling a list of grievances and see how God has used these moments of desperation in your life to clear a path for some much needed grace.

The lesson I learned that day in wood shop has turned up in other ways since high school. What I mean is: People are going to fail; I am going to fail; you are going to fail; we are going to fail. Show me someone who does not appear to fail, and I will show you someone distracted by maintaining an ego driven by appearance over vulnerable authenticity. Sometimes failures are big, ugly, and public, leaving behind visible and permanent scars. Other times they are private but equally painful. On a few occasions, it will look like someone even failed on purpose because the idea was so bad or conduct so outrageous it is hard to conceive of it being merely a mistake. The fact is, most people don't aim to fail. Sometimes we just forget who we are for a little while. We forget the rules and boundaries we set for ourselves. We listen to lesser voices and find ourselves agreeing for a moment. We forget the poosh stick, and we pay the price. Sometimes the people we love the most pay the price too.

We do the same with God. I don't know many people who set out to disappoint God, yet we all do at some point. But here's the thing: When we make a mistake, we have a chance to take His grace out for a drive. Even the origins of the word *grace* in Hebrew point us in a beautiful direction. Imagine pitching a tent in the middle of an area surrounded and protected by a wall of other tents closely bunched together. Grace isn't about a "do-over"; it's about protection. Our failures remind us of our desperate need for more grace and heavenly help, not less of it. Our failures reinforce the important and worthwhile purposes we are trying to live out because, if we didn't care so much, we wouldn't see our blunders as failures to begin with.

The challenge is this: What will you believe about yourself after a failure? Will you assume you have crashed and burned in someone else's prescription for your life? Will you bail on doing the one thing God uniquely put in front of you to master, even though you muffed it the first time? Will you let approval and applause be your barometer for success, purpose, and meaning? Or will you see and aim for something different, something more beautiful that God has prepared you for?

––––––––

Ever since she was a little longer than a trout, I've been telling my daughter, Lindsey, that a guy would want to marry her someday. I told her if I liked the guy, I would invite him along with my other sons to build a chapel at our place in Canada for their wedding. I also told her if I didn't like the guy, we wouldn't get around to it.

An amazing young man named Jon came onto the scene in my daughter's life. Within a short while, their relationship blossomed, and we could all see where it was headed. Jon is a humble, brilliant soul. He is kind and thoughtful, loves God, and is incredibly deliberate and focused in everything he does.

Jon asked Sweet Maria and me to meet one Saturday. Sitting around on the back patio, he described what Lindsey meant to him and how he wanted to spend his life learning more about the depths of her beautiful heart. As a parent, you dream about this day and the one who will be on the other side of this conversation. You hope for someone as magnificent as Jon. Temper your expectations because you can't control such things. Between you and me, I was thrilled about Jon, but as a dad I felt like I needed to fake a good poker face.

After all, Lindsey is my only daughter, so this conversation would be both the practice and the performance for the only son-in-law slot I have available.

We listened intently as he said he loved Lindsey and asked us for our blessing on the decision they had already made to get married. "Well, I don't know," I said as I looked him up and down a little, just to make him squirm. (He didn't. He could stare down a panther.) "Can you swing a hammer?"

"Huh?" he said.

Lindsey didn't need a building to know her dad and family loved her. Honestly, she didn't even want one. Do you know why we built it? Because I wanted a son-in-law who was a friend, not someone I needed to just be polite to. I wanted Lindsey to partner with someone who delighted in being part of what we were building as a family. I wanted to learn from Jon about the power of purpose in his own life and how he swept aside all other distractions to chase it.

One day early into the project it was time do a bunch of rip cuts to get our beams ready for the side walls. To do a rip cut you need a table saw. Jon and I walked over, and I flipped on the switch. The air filled with loud whirs and microscopic wood dust from our past work. We hoisted the first piece of lumber onto the table, and Jon began to push. When his fingers got somewhat close to the blade, he stopped and got a scrap piece of wood to push it through. I immediately thought of Mr. Hodgkins, the wisdom I learned from him, and the confidence I had in Jon. He got the poosh stick.

Here's the crazy thing. We didn't finish the chapel in time, and Jon and Lindsey got married under an arbor Jon built by himself and covered with branches. They liked it way better than any building I could have dreamed up. Still, working on the chapel as a family will forever remain one of my favorite memories. Before we finished the interior walls, we had friends up to the Lodge and we all wrote prayers and messages of hope and purpose on the framing for our family and future generations. Every time I step into that space, I can hear them whispering the truths about pursuing God's purposes in our lives without distraction.

The only script God has for us is Jesus. He doesn't care about your alma mater or who you voted for or what your position is on the big topic of the day. He doesn't care what's in your bank account or whether you lead from in front or behind at a church. He doesn't even care if you work at Disneyland. His only measuring stick for you is His Son, whom He loves. What is unimaginably and inexplicably beautiful is that God loves you and me with that *same love* He has for His Son, in equal measure, without comparison, until the end of time and beyond. It's hard to get my arms or my fingers around that kind of math. So why care about the grades your best friend makes or the car your neighbor drives? Why carry around those negative predictions and proclamations from the doubters? Get busy seeing yourself the way God sees you. Sure, you might hit a few snags along the way. Some of them might take a chunk out of you. But when we live on purpose, with joy, and without distraction, we will ditch the invisible scoreboard we have been tempted to live by. If we do this, distractions will lose their power over us, and we will cultivate a caring community who won't shake their heads in disapproval when we mess up. Instead they will remind us of our purpose and potential.

CHAPTER 6

ALL-ACCESS PASS

God gave you all the permission you need, so don't get distracted looking for it from everyone else.

It was Texas in the 1980s, and a couple was having a relaxed Saturday morning strolling through a garage sale in a nearby neighborhood. They loved seeing the little knickknacks and discarded treasures. As they ambled around the makeshift tables, the husband glanced at a *very* used guitar hidden by a heap of polyester clothes. He thought his oldest son would like it, so he haggled a five-dollar price tag and brought home the raggedy instrument. The oldest boy wasn't really that into it, so he passed the guitar on to his little brother, Ed, who grabbed the guitar with a kind of reverence. A dream was kindled inside of him.

Ever since first gripping the neck of that guitar, Ed dreamed of being a world-famous musician. He practiced and worked for years and years. He played in dive joints and with many different bands just to build his experience. It wasn't long before Ed got pretty good and started playing shows at larger venues. By the time he was in his twenties, he was dazzling crowds with his electric guitar. At about the same time, he met a young country western singer who was putting a band together. Her name was Carrie Underwood. Ed was invited to join the band, and for the next twenty years he toured the world with Carrie and melted faces with his guitar and his incredibly kind heart.

Ed called me to say they were swinging through San Diego on their worldwide tour and asked if I wanted a ticket. "Heck yeah," I immediately said. The show was sold out and I looked online to see how much a ticket would cost. Even the cheapest seat in the place was more expensive than dinner for four, so I was glad he offered me a free one. The instructions Ed gave me to get into the show were simple: Go to the will-call booth, claim the ticket, and find your seat. How hard could that be?

As I approached the arena, the atmosphere was electric. People were lined up in a huge queue to get in; they were in a good mood and excited about the fun evening ahead. I was excited to have the chance to see my friend doing what he does best, and I had a big grin on my face as I approached will-call and picked up the envelope with my name on it. With my ticket in hand, I got through the entrance and started making my way to the nosebleed seats. I figured they wouldn't have any uber-expensive front-row tickets just lying around. I didn't mind though. I was stoked just to be in the arena. *This is going to be awesome*, I thought to myself as I climbed the many flights of stairs to my seat up in the rafters.

At the top of the stairs on the upper level, a guy with a flashlight stopped me and inspected my ticket. "This isn't a ticket for this section," he said. "You need to head down to the main floor. Once you're down there, find someone who looks like me and they'll point you in the right direction." I was excited about this seat upgrade and thought that was really nice of Ed to get me a little closer to the stage. I skipped down toward the main floor with even more anticipation.

When I got there, another usher stopped me and took a close look at my ticket. "You're in the wrong section, buddy," he said, grinning. I wondered if maybe the guy up top had made a mistake and I was about to climb all those stairs again. If that happened, I told myself to look on the bright side and think of it as good exercise. *At least I'll get my steps in for the day.* But instead of pointing back up, he pointed farther in toward the stage. "This ticket will get you into the area inside that second stage over there. The kids these days call it a mosh pit."

"Really?" I said, surprised by the news. He was pointing at an oval stage connected by a walkway to the main stage. People were filling up the space inside the oval where the band would come out at some point and play some songs. Things were really going my way. I had gone from the nosebleed section all the way to the mosh pit. Then again, I had no idea what a mosh pit was. What is mosh anyway? And if you get some on you, how would you know and how would you get it off? Maybe I could put some white vinegar on it and soak myself overnight? I figured I would find out. "Let's mosh it up!" I said as I pressed my way through the crowd toward the stage.

I can't lie—as I approached the mosh pit, it looked pretty rowdy. Kind of like people in a blender just after someone turned the dial to *liquefy* and flipped the switch. There was a person standing at the entrance who asked to see my ticket. I sheepishly held it out, once again wondering if the guy before had made a mistake. If I made it in, I would be one of the few old guys in the mosh pit, and I was starting to look forward to the experience. Jesus, take the wheel, right? The guy looked at the ticket once, then again with his flashlight. Then he got another security guard close by to look at the ticket and verify its authenticity. He looked up at me and laughed. "Buddy, this is an all-access pass. You can go anywhere with this thing." I wondered if it would be overstepping to head back to Carrie's tour bus and make myself a sandwich.

Getting me a ticket was so kind of everyone in the band. Not only did they get me in the building; they also made it possible for me to go anywhere I wanted while I was there. The thing is, I didn't realize I had that kind of permission in my hands. It took three burly security guards to convince me I had far more access than I really believed, imagined, or understood. My gracious hosts wanted me to have whatever vantage point I chose. I could certainly have looked on from afar if I wanted to, but I was also invited right into the mix. The only place I couldn't go that night was to the center of the stage.

Perhaps this is what God wants you to know as well. He's given you access to go anywhere with your life and the whole world to do it in. The only spot that's already taken is center stage, where Jesus already has it covered.

Sometimes people make faith complicated, but the invitation Jesus gave us is not: We have an all-access pass, and all we need to do is show up and claim it. But using an all-access pass takes a good dose of boldness. If you want the freedom to go anywhere, a mindset shift has to take place. No one is the gatekeeper of our lives and our joy anymore. We also need to permanently set aside asking for permission to live into what God has already placed in our hearts and told us to release into the world. In short, we have already been invited into our beautiful lives, so we don't have to wonder if this is where we really belong or have the right to be.

If you are ready to claim your all-access pass, I need to warn you: Living with boldness can make other people a little uncomfortable. Here's why. People who are still asking for permission get antsy when they see this kind of unbridled agency and vision in motion. They see a rule-breaker when they see anyone brazen enough to tear down the manufactured barrier between life-as-it-is and life-as-it-could-be. Maybe they also wish they had that kind of courage. Who knows? So, will it be hard at times to live this way? You bet. Will you be turned away by some people or become disappointed by circumstances and surprises along the way? Of course you will. Will you be confused at times about where the adventure is taking you? You can bank on it.

You can expect some confusion, too, because having an all-access pass means not everything will be spelled out for you. You will probably also have to unlearn the pronouncements made at some point by the cynical, ill-informed, or disillusioned people who have intersected your life. Do these sound familiar? *You're not smart enough. You're not capable enough. Who do you think you are to be doing this? You don't have what it takes. It's not worth it.* (Read: *You're not worth it.*) *Why are you taking this crazy risk? Don't you see you're going to fail?*

Some of us might need to ask ourselves why we keep heading for the predictability and obscurity of the rafters rather than moving a little closer to the action. Sure, we can play it safe and head for the faraway places. The Scriptures say that even the disciples looked on from far away at times.[1] If we do, we might be able to take a selfie and even say we were in the arena somewhere. Or we can take God up on His invitation to a much less predictable path—the one filled with an eclectic gaggle of people living out their faith in the mosh pit. Figuring out where your unique ticket lets you go might require asking yourself what you want to do with your life, then summoning the guts and grit you'll need to accept the permission God has already put in your hand. The truth is, everyone will face barriers, and the world is full of baubles and trinkets and naysayers and systemic pressures and injustices and misguided dreams that can take us off the path. An all-access pass isn't a cheat code for any easy life; it's the key for a purposeful and more joyful one.

Vesta Stoudt claimed her ticket and is an example of a woman filled with purpose. She worked in a factory in Illinois during World War II. She inspected ammunition boxes and noticed a major flaw. The boxes at the time were sealed with paper and a pull tab, but the paper tab would get soaked and allow water into the container. This ruined the ammo, so the soldiers would dip the boxes in wax to keep everything dry. Problem was, the wax made it much harder to access the ammo, which is more than an inconvenience when fumbling with an ammo box during intense firefights could cost someone their life.

Vesta had two sons in the military, and she knew plenty of other families with enlisted soldiers too. She wanted them all to get what they needed for the fights they were in. She didn't just stay concerned; she got busy. She realized she had permission to create and innovate, so she dove into the immense task of trying to fix the problem she saw. She drew diagrams and made samples to fix the ammo boxes. When her work was complete, she prepared a presentation for her supervisors to get their support. She was convinced her invention of a sticky tape could save many lives. Unfortunately, her boss thought it was a lousy idea. I'm sure he wasn't a bad guy—maybe just a person who didn't get it. Why create a waterproof fabric tape? Lesson one here: Don't let your great idea wither as you wait for approval.

Vesta didn't take no for an answer when her idea wasn't well-received, and she wasn't going to wait for approval from someone who didn't see her vision. She knew why she was doing what she was doing. She wanted her sons to have what they needed and refused to get knocked off course by the person who had authority over her job but not her life.[2] That's the kind of boldness I'm talking about. She was filled with intention, and she was determined. Can you find this power in your life? Can you give your God-given creativity this kind of unstoppable license?

In the business world, it's a big deal if you go above your boss to make a request, especially when that boss already has shut the door in your face. Well, Vesta didn't just go to her boss's boss; she went to the president of the United States. This is exactly the kind of leap we're talking about. She sent a letter to President Roosevelt that included her idea and a sample. Then she asked for approval to manufacture what she had dreamed up so people could fight the fights they were in.[3]

I wish I could have been there when the letter arrived from the War Production Board. Her idea was approved for immediate production. And get this: Vesta Stoudt's idea and work led to the invention of duct tape. I'm not kidding. One woman refused to believe she needed permission to follow her gut and her imagination. She made some bold moves to see it through. It didn't matter to her that others couldn't understand, didn't approve, or didn't see the need for her idea. She wasn't looking for approval; she was focused on the possibilities.

Today, the military still uses duct tape for all kinds of applications. One of its unofficial names is "100-mph tape" because it has been used it to patch Jeep bumpers and even helicopter rotor blades. They also use it to patch worn-out boots and straps on packs. No space shot by NASA has ever left the earth without a roll or two of duct tape. You name it, and duct tape does it. As the saying goes: "If you can't fix it with duct tape, you need more duct tape."

Love and acceptance will work much the same way in your life. If you can't fix the circumstance you are in with purpose and joy, you probably need more Jesus. An undistracted life filled with love and joy and purpose and faith might just be the duct tape you need to hold your dreams together.

Let me confirm for you what you have suspected for a long time. You have permission to pursue your beautiful ideas and interests. (Unless you want to knock off liquor stores. In that case, then not so much.) You have permission to go deeper in your relationships with God and with the fallible people He made. You have permission to quit the career you are merely capable of and trade it in for the one you have been hoping for. You have permission to be twice as real as you have been, and you definitely have my express permission to invent the next version of a cake pop and send me a case or two.

Don't get distracted by the safety of the familiar or by the scripts and expectations everyone else has for your life. Friends, parents, pastors, and spouses all mean well. But if you want to dazzle God, stop thinking you need a different ticket than the one you've already got. Stop waiting for someone to say you have permission to pursue your ideas or your beautiful and lasting ambitions. Go live fully. Heaven can't wait to see what you'll do when you show up each day with your all-access pass. Your existence—your one beautiful and brief life—is the only ticket you need. It's right there in your hand already.

CHAPTER 7

JESUS IN THE ROOM

God has already given us the waypoints
to find a life of purpose.

I've sailed to and from Hawaii a couple of times. I'm planning to do it again soon, though I'm not sure why I keep doing it, really. I spend most of the time on the high seas hurling over the side. I drop about twenty pounds every time, so there's that. It's kind of like a really messy weight-loss program where you eat the food once and see it twice. The trip to Hawaii from San Diego is about twenty-six hundred miles, give or take a palm tree, which is a long way by any measure. If you think of your life span as a trip from California to the Big Island, you can imagine how it wouldn't happen in one straight line and without some rough water along the way. You also wouldn't just set sail from San Diego without a plan and some indications that you are headed in the right direction.

When you're on a long journey, the shorter legs are divided by waypoints. Having intermediate points along a route helps you chart your progress toward a longer-range goal. When you're close to land, a waypoint can be something like a lighthouse, a distinct piece of coastline, or a mountaintop. Waypoints on the open sea are a little harder to come by and aren't nearly as reliable. You can't get to Hawaii by taking a left at the first dolphin fin or piece of kelp you pass. So sailors use points of latitude and longitude to mark a position and chart their path toward it. They also use these points to communicate their location to others. Waypoints are crucial because it's easy to drift or feel numbed by the vast nothingness of the ocean's surface. You need something solid and unchanging to steer toward if you want to complete the journey.

Think of the waypoints of your life as a series of all the things you have been aiming toward, for whatever number of days you have been here. Perhaps these have been things like jobs or relationships or items you have accumulated. Now, think about all the things you want to pursue for the days you have left. Being undistracted means staying the course with things that will outlast you. It's a long journey, and the trick is to find some waypoints that matter and are a little closer together than the ones you have been pointing toward.

To be sure, wanting to "live a good life" is a wonderful ambition and worthy of your aim; but accomplishing this might be a long distance between where you are today and where you will want to be when you cross heaven's starting line. Here's my suggestion: Chunk it up a little. Have a conversation with yourself and perhaps some trusted friends about what constitutes a good, purposeful, and joy-filled life. Focus on a few of those things and try to make one or two moves in their direction every day. Repeat this practice for fifty years, and I promise you will have "lived a good life." It won't be good luck, a lottery ticket, or a sleight of hand, but rather hourly, undistracted focus and several good daily habits that will get you there. Perhaps this is why God only gave the Israelites one day's worth of food at a time and why Jesus taught His friends to pray for their *daily* bread and not a lifetime's worth all at once.[1]

Did you know you can actually drift to Hawaii—or at least try to—if you have a vessel that won't sink? I don't recommend doing this for a vacation or as a way to live your life, but if you decide to drift to the islands, there is a current just off Cabo San Lucas, Mexico, that will take you west at ten inches a minute. This is pretty fast if you're moving from one side of the couch to the other, but if you're crossing an ocean, this pace will let you down. It will take months, and even then, you will pass hundreds of miles south of the island chain. You won't even see a volcano or a coconut tree as you pass by.

Here is what I'm getting at. A slow drift in a general direction probably isn't going to get you where you want to go in your life, nor will it get you anywhere quickly. Distractions are not riptides. They are slow-moving currents that will lead you away from your ambitions, relationships, and joy every time.

It doesn't matter what age you are. Now is the perfect time to drill down and get clear on what you are actually aiming for if you want to have any hope of coming close to it. Merely telling yourself in general terms that you are going to "head west" won't work either. West is a big place, and versions of it include everything but what is to the east. Instead, navigate toward something a little more precise and worthy of the trip if you want to arrive at a meaningful destination. Start by naming the purposeful things in your life that will go the distance—things like faith, hope, and love.[2] These are the things Jesus said would outlast everything else. Once you have identified these things in your life, don't stop there; get busy taking aim at them.

My ultimate hope for us is that we will decide to set sail rather than wait for the right time to untie from the dock. Then set a purposeful course forward with the wind at your back and joy in your heart, and don't settle for the slow drift. Keep this one thing in mind: Only dead fish go with the flow. Don't be one of them. People who accomplish a great deal in their lives are filled with joy and lasting ambitions; they choose a direction, then take the steps and actions needed to stay the course. Be one of these people, and you will find your joy once again.

Setting sail isn't enough though. Don't get distracted by the false positive of empty productivity. Activity can punk you into believing you are making progress when you aren't, and busyness can look purposeful when it's really just a bunch of nervous, unbridled energy. Why not decide right now to trade in all the frenetic activity you have been medicating yourself with? Trade it in for a worthy destination, clarity of direction, confidence in the permission you already have, resolve to stay the course, and joy for the journey. Rest assured, more than a few unanticipated things are going to happen along the way—so knowing why you are doing what you are doing is critical.

I have a friend who made the trip from Hawaii to Seattle a few years before I set sail for the first time, so I asked him for some tips. He told me that all the preparation is necessary—as you would suspect—but so is a level head and a checklist you can confidently work your way through so you don't forget something important.

Have you ever slept through an alarm the morning you are supposed to catch a flight? You end up tossing a bunch of stuff into a bag and hoping you got it all before dashing out the door. This can happen to anyone. My friend's departure from Ala Wai Harbor on Oahu was a little bit like this. He was incredibly rushed, and his last frantic act was to top off the fuel and the water on the boat before beginning his ocean crossing. This was a perfectly good thing to do for such a long journey. A few days out to sea, however, they pulled some water from the storage tank, and it tasted pretty bad. In his haste, my friend had accidentally topped off the water tank with diesel fuel and the diesel tank with water.

My friend's simple and rushed mistake eventually had some big real-world consequences. Because there was diesel in the water, they couldn't really drink it. As a result, they ate a lot of canned peaches. This had some predictable results, and they ended up being awfully busy below decks. That was a big problem but not the only one. Because there was water in the diesel, the engine stopped. Because the engine stopped, the batteries couldn't charge and eventually went dead. Because there were no batteries, they had no way to radio for help, and they lost the electronic navigation equipment needed to verify their waypoints. Their only option was to head in a general direction and navigate as best they could under the circumstances.

They survived the trip, but they missed their destination by hundreds of miles. Don't let distraction set in motion this kind of cascade effect of unintended consequences for your life.

There's another form of drifting that is less about our decisions and more about our relationships and our faith. I have a few friends who are world-class musicians, and they perform on some pretty big stages. Whenever they are in my town or we happen to intersect when I'm traveling, I try to go to their shows. I love seeing people glowing with their gifts, and live music is such a fun way to experience that. So when a friend of mine invited me to his show, it was an easy yes—and I arrived early so I could get some time with him in the greenroom beforehand.

This particular evening, more than a thousand people waited excitedly at the venue for the concert to begin. Behind the stage a few band members were in the room while my friend and I caught up and laughed about some of the adventures we had shared over the years. We had gotten into plenty of mischief and had lots to talk about. After a few minutes I glanced to my right and noticed a guy sitting by himself at the end of the table. He sat with his hands folded in his lap, and he had a peaceful grin on his face as he looked in our direction. I guessed he was a friend of someone in the band because everyone seemed to know him.

Sometimes people try to wedge their way into conversation, but the guy at the end of the table just sat there, smiling. He also had the most piercing blue eyes I'd ever seen. Since Sweet Maria's eyes aren't blue, I feel okay saying that. At one point we made accidental eye contact, and it felt like he was looking straight into my soul. It was both arresting and uncomfortable, and I took a mental note to inquire about colored contacts if I ever wanted to have this effect on people.

Eventually the band needed to take the stage, and we said our goodbyes. Someone escorted me and the guy with the blue eyes down a hallway and showed us how we could slip into the venue through a side door. We tried to be discreet as we took our seats, and nobody cared when I entered the room. But when the people saw the guy I walked in with, they started poking each other and pointing in his direction. I was a little embarrassed that I was so out of touch but tried to play it cool. I sank into my seat as quickly as possible.

I didn't know until my seat neighbor told me that the blue-eyed guy was Jim Caviezel, the actor best known for his role as the Messiah in *The Passion of the Christ*. I chuckled to myself, realizing I had been in a room with Jesus for almost an hour and didn't even know it. Perhaps you can relate.

While this is a cute little story, you probably already know where I'm going with it. How many times have we failed to realize Jesus is in the room with us? We live much of our lives unaware, drifting in our own way toward God, not realizing that He's already right there beside us and has been there for a long time. Distraction steals our awareness, and living this way steals our joy. This, of course, is no surprise to Jesus; He knew it would happen to us because He saw it happening to the people around Him. Some of His friends knew who He was, but when asked, they pretended they didn't. This didn't fool anyone, including the nearby rooster. Others passed by Jesus on the street never knowing it was Him.[3]

Think about it for a second. This pattern started when Jesus was young and was surrounded by the religious people in a synagogue. "Who is this kid? Why does He speak with so much authority?" they wondered.[4] It happened again at a wedding surrounded by friends and family who asked Him to fix a problem He didn't create.[5] It happened on a cross, flanked by two criminals, and it occurred again next to an empty tomb when Mary mistook Him for a gardener. Even His close friends didn't recognize Him the next day on a shoreline, or a little later along the road to Emmaus.[6]

Jesus didn't want to be a mystery. He didn't try to hide His identity then, and He's still not in that business. I bet He knows that those of us distracted or scared or confused or obsessing about something else simply wouldn't notice Him in the room. People like you and people like me still miss Him all the time. Nevertheless, He promised that the ones who really look for Him will find Him; the ones who cry out for Him will be given what they really need and find both joy and purpose in their lives.

Jesus left us some clear waypoints to His location. Finding Jesus is not like following a set of hidden geocaching clues; instead, He's dropping us a pin on a map with His exact location. He told us wherever there are hungry people or thirsty people, He would be there. Anywhere someone is sick or estranged or naked or in jail. He didn't ask us to do Him a solid by reaching out to people in distress; He promised we would actually find *Him* when we tried to meet their needs. He said He would be present with the widows and the orphans. Wherever two or more of His people gather in His name, He said He'd be in that room too.[7]

The problem for you is probably the same problem I have all the time. We are so distracted by the things happening *around* us that we overlook what God could be doing *within* us. The fix is both easy and hard. We need to connect the dots from what we have heard *about* our faith to what we actually do *with* our faith. This confusion doesn't come from a bad place necessarily, and I find myself mixing them up all the time. Here's why. Somewhere along the way, we probably got distracted by everything that competes for our attention.

We need to realign, refine, and reconnect with the greater purposes for our lives rather than be distracted by the lesser ones. We need to swivel our heads to look for opportunities right in front of us rather than fixating on the ones behind us. You'll know this strategy is working when you start noticing the needs of the people around you and using the margin in your life to take on a couple of them. Stop leaving this as an academic exercise; make it personal. It's not about merely gathering a greater amount of information or thinking about a new program for your faith community; it's about developing a greater awareness of what is already happening around us and showing up for it with a boatload of joy and anticipation.

The average person lives about 27,375 days.[8] Fewer if you eat salt-water taffy, and a few more if you eat broccoli. How we spend our days can have incredible ramifications for good or for ill in the world. Let's not spend a ridiculous number of them on distractions that steal our joy.

Twenty-seven thousand days sounds like a big number to some people and a small number to guys like me who have twenty-three thousand in the rearview mirror. I don't know where you fall on that timeline, but here is something I want you to consider. How much do you truly value and cherish your time? Do you look at each day as a precious contribution to your future, or are you content just meandering aimlessly through your weeks? Are you content with trying not to rock the boat, which happens when we take risks, or are you willing to build the sides of the boat a little higher so the water doesn't swamp you when you do? Do you have a clear destination and established waypoints? If you don't, now is your time. It's too easy to fall into the trap of deferral by replacing intention and focus with distraction and apathy. Remember this: We will become in our lives what we do with our love.

How many days remain for you? Do the math. Who will you decide to be, and what will you decide to do with the time you have left? We can spend our remaining days focused on the meaningful and beautiful and joyous and purposeful, or we can drift aimlessly and fritter away our one wild and precious life. One of the astounding gifts of God is that the choice is ours to make. We can get busy right now throwing our energy into things that matter.

Here's more good news: There is a surefire way to get clear on all of this. Find Jesus wherever you are. Use Him as your starting and ending points, then find some waypoints in the middle you can depend on. Stop pining away your days waiting for God to show up; He's already in the room. You can stop telling yourself you are waiting on Him because He's probably waiting on you.

CHAPTER 8

NO STALKING, PLEASE

If we learn truth without acting on it, we turn a Savior into a mere teacher.

I've written a few books that people have read and (hopefully) enjoyed. I have relished the opportunity to write some stories and hear how they help people. I also take little snippets of my ideas and put them on social media. To me it feels like a communal conversation where I get to put out the starter prompt and delight in watching others bake it into something better. All of this has been really wonderful, for the most part.

Sweet Maria and I lead a fairly quiet life despite how much I wave my arms around and get excited. So it got really creepy when people triangulated my address from the description of my house in my books. One morning I woke up early and walked downstairs to turn on the coffee. There was a guy sitting on the other side of the window on my back porch. I opened my back door and said, "Hi, who are you?" You can always tell someone's a stalker because the first thing they often say is, "I'm not a stalker." *All evidence to the contrary*, I thought. Another time I arrived home late from the airport, changed into my favorite blue shirt and sweatpants, and walked into the living room where Sweet Maria was reading. My phone rang as I stood near the window, and a woman said, "That's a nice blue shirt you have on." It could've been Betty White calling me, and she still would've sounded like a serial killer with a line like that. I didn't say anything in response; I just pulled the blinds and nervously hung up. She was standing on our lawn looking in the window.

This kind of thing happens when I'm out and about too. One time I was on a late flight back home to San Diego. I had already crisscrossed the country a few times that week, and it is my personal rule to always try to get home to Sweet Maria in the evening when I can. When my speaking schedule has been packed, I can go to Atlanta and back in a day and some variation of that trip four days a week. I have *a lot* of frequent-flyer miles. So on this particular flight, after a long week, I had settled into my seat and closed my eyes. As soon as I let out a deep exhale, I felt something on my lap. *Maybe a seatmate is putting their bag in my lap before lifting it into the overhead bin.* I knew that would be a little odd but decided to let it go and try to project a serene, uninterested calm. Actually, what I really tried to project was: *I'm sleeping, so please get your stuff off my lap.* Then I started hearing keyboard taps like someone was typing on a computer.

When I opened my eyes, I saw that a dude had set his laptop, well, on my lap. Ironic, I suppose. Anyway, he said he recognized me from a talk I gave at his church. He evidently really liked my books and thought it would be okay for him to contact his girlfriend via FaceTime to join this special event he was hosting in my seat. I was the special guest, except I had never been invited or accepted the invite.

Pro tip here: Don't do that.

Okay, last one. I got a message on Twitter from a guy in Texas who heard I would be passing through Dallas in two weeks. He wanted to meet. I was grateful for the invitation, but told him I was landing at Dallas Love Field, so I wouldn't be able to make it. I didn't hear anything more from him.

Two weeks later, I was heading to Dallas. It just so happened my friend John, whom I hadn't seen in years, was passing through as well. He was on some kind of cross-country road trip that started in his hometown near Washington DC. To have a chance to see my friend, I asked if he would want to give me a ride to my hotel once I landed in Dallas. Our schedules perfectly aligned, and he said he would pick me up at 10:00 p.m. in a Suburban.

Everything worked like a Swiss clock. I deplaned, made my way to baggage claim, and stepped out of the terminal at 10:00 p.m. At 10:01 John pulled up in his Suburban and called out to me, "Bob!" I walked across a few lanes of traffic and looked in the passenger window. Honestly, John didn't look like what I remembered, but it had been several years and I thought maybe he had changed his diet or something. Still, I'm no dummy, so I asked him a vetting question: "How was the drive from DC?" Without missing a beat, he said, "It was a snap. Just took a couple of days." So I got in the car and we started driving.

We were about five miles from the airport when I got a text message on my phone. It said, "Bob, I'm at the airport. Where are you?" I read it twice as it started sinking in that I wasn't in the car with John. I turned to the guy behind the wheel, my eyes big like saucers, and stammered, "You're not John, are you?" I tried to sound confident, but I think my voice cracked a little. "No, I'm not," he said slowly with his eyes weirdly glazed. *Yikes.*

Then I recalled my brief exchange on Twitter from a couple of weeks before. It was Twitter Dude! And he had a Suburban! What were the chances? "I'm the guy who messaged you," he said as I reached for the door handle, wondering if we were going too fast for me to safely roll out onto the pavement. "Of course you are," was all I could muster through a clenched smile.

I had him pull over so I could catch my other ride. When I got out, I asked him, "What's the deal saying you drove here from DC?" He looked surprised and said, "I moved here from DC three years ago." This was all too weird, and I found out a little more about him. Get this. This guy was a Juilliard-trained musician who wanted to teach our students in Northern Uganda how to play music. He decided he had to meet me first, so Twitter Dude just went to the airport and started circling, waiting for me to come outside. He didn't mean to be creepy; he just *was* creepy. Perhaps he had just spent a little too much time with his sheet music in a dark and windowless room. Who knows?

Everyone I've described here distracted me in some way. They didn't mean to, but they still did. You may not have someone lurking outside your living room window, but I bet you have people in your life who think they're entitled to your time, energy, ideas, output, input, and everything else in between. They text you, call you, Vox you, TikTok you, and hit you up on the DMs until they get a reply. They think their persistence is a virtue, when what they're really doing is annoying you and failing to "read the room." They are looking at your life through the lens of their needs, not yours. I suppose we all do that to some degree. If such folks have become a distraction for you or are making off with your joy, you have my permission to not call them back. Don't answer the email. It may feel weird and a little rude, but it's not. You're establishing boundaries for yourself. You are reminding yourself that a long string of distractions can become a lifetime of uncompleted visions. Keep in mind what Solomon said: "Above all else, guard your heart, for everything you do flows from it."[1] They will figure out some other way to connect with someone else who can be available to them.

If you feel you are getting too many unsolicited knocks at your door, you may need to consider the kind of signals you are putting out and the kinds of boundaries you are erecting (or not, as the case may be). You need to do this carefully because setting boundaries is not an all-or-nothing proposition. Think of it this way. Boundaries are good; barriers aren't. If you build a wall, make sure you install a door or two. If you want a moat, don't forget the drawbridge. Why? Because if you deny *all* access, even when it is inconvenient or unwanted, you will find yourself more than alone. Instead you will be isolated. You sometimes need serendipitous points of input and accidental meetings to find the kismet and providence that bring your beautiful life into focus.

Are you a pastor of a big church and yet separated from everyone? How come? We don't need to graft business and celebrity culture into our faith communities, but you can go to the front door and hand out some saltwater taffy. Even if your sermon is lousy, people will feel the love of God expressed through these acts of purposeful kindness and availability. Give people a way in or get a job doing something else. I know your time is important, but try being wonderfully inefficient in the way you love the people around you. If you wrote a song or a book or showed up in a movie or two, don't become unavailable to people. Find the right way to let a few people across the moat while safeguarding the amount of privacy your heart, not your ego, says you need. Don't let your rock-star status become a distraction to you or to the people who look up to you. You are only one generous act of availability away from being a better version of yourself.

I think it's immensely important we get this balance right in our relationships. We also need some balance when it comes to our relationship with Jesus.

Have you been stalking Jesus? Have you memorized verses and learned the location of every Bible story? Do you know all the Bible names and genealogies? Can you recite what Jesus said to a crowd and then walk a stranger down the "Roman Road"? Have you been in church so long that you forgot how to communicate with the guy at the tire store who would only go if he lost a bet?

Stalking Jesus looks like a bunch of knowledge without an equal portion of action. (Maybe you're thinking of the book of James here.) At some point in my life of faith I realized I *knew* plenty of things about Jesus but hadn't actually *done* anything with Jesus. I was like a professor who taught the class but wasn't a practitioner. I knew the verses about the poor and the widows and the orphans. Meanwhile I had never done a single thing to be like Jesus to them. I guess you could say donating money or tithing inched me closer to that. But I don't see in the Bible where we are exempted from getting involved in these needs because we tossed some money in the direction of the poor. Don't get me wrong; we need to be stewards of our resources by pouring into what God cares about. However, money is not the same as serving; each of these can be acts of worship if done well, changing your heart in different ways. What I mean is, we need both. We need to spend more time doing the things Jesus told us to do than we do merely talking about them. In other words, we need to stop stalking Jesus.

Sometimes I'm asked this question: "Where should I start?" Here's my answer: It doesn't matter. Here, there, down the street, under the bridge, in Singapore, on ice skates, or in a hot-air balloon. The people who live wildly purposeful and joy-filled lives act first and ask questions later. They know that concocting a master plan can really be just a distraction in disguise. They realize that by the time they are finished with the planning and fundraising they could have just started the project instead.

If you need a starting nudge, maybe the best first step is to find what you trust the most and put wheels on it. If you are a Jesus person, what you trust might be what you find in the books and letters compiled into the Bible—words that will give you more than a lifetime of ideas for how to live a more joyful and purposeful life. If faith isn't your thing, then find something else you can put your trust in. Who knows? Perhaps the answer will come later. I have a habit each morning. After I make the coffee, I have time to focus and reflect. Some faith communities call this a "quiet time." The truth is, I haven't had a quiet time in twenty years, at least not in the way some people think of it. I do something similar, but it's actually a really loud time to me. I use the time to true up the things I believe are right and then search the Bible to see if they square with what Scripture says. For me it's a time to be alone and to enjoy God, not an appointment I feel obligated to keep.

For years I would wash Sweet Maria's car in the morning. The practice helped me clear away the distractions in my busy life. This was part of my quiet time. I would think and reflect on things Jesus said and figure out what to do about the more difficult things He commanded, such as loving my enemies and helping those in need. I took merely agreeing with Him off the table. If there was something I really needed to lean into, I would stay in the driveway a little longer and wash Sweet Maria's wheels and rims. Because I spent many loud hours with Jesus in the mornings, Sweet Maria's car was always spotless. Find something that works for you. When it stops working, find something new. I'll have my car out by the curb if you need a project.

I think some people in our faith communities have quiet times because someone told them they were supposed to. Then if they don't make time, they feel guilty. God never mentions quiet time in the Bible, and frankly, I don't think He cares if we have it or not. What I think He wants is for us to spend undistracted time with Him all the time. If morning is your time to read and reflect, terrific. If not, find another time. Whenever it happens, make it as loud or as quiet as you need it to be to propel you forward. If the traditions, structures, and practices your faith community came up with don't help you surround your life with Jesus, scrap them and come up with something better for you. I wouldn't want someone to spend time with me because they would feel guilty if they didn't. I don't think God wants us to do that either. I bet He would rather be with us riding a Ferris wheel or a skateboard or playing the cello than sitting with Him like we are in detention.

As part of my daily reflections, I write down my thoughts one sentence at a time and then email them to myself. I get more than one hundred emails a day from this guy named Bob. I'm thinking about blocking him. The next morning, I revisit these thoughts to see if they sound right or if they are actually true. Do this kind of sorting and resorting in your life as often as possible. You'll understand yourself and your faith better if you do. I've emailed myself things that were beautiful and pointed toward the truths in the Scriptures. Some become my social media posts. Other things I write down sound right but don't end up squaring with Scripture, and you will never see these repeated by me.

The reason I read Scripture in the morning is because I'm hoping to have a little more truth to help me combat the distractions in my life. I never know what the day holds for me. None of us knows. My time in the morning helps me to wireframe my day in advance with truth and perspective and love. It's like putting some empty clothes hangers in the closet, so that when life hands me some unexpected circumstances, I have a place to hang them. I'd rather take a good look at them later than leave them in a pile on the floor.

It's funny how we can sniff out a stalker pretty easily. There is just something about them that sets off our radars. Here's the thing. Maybe God is looking at us the same way, saying, "The pot is calling the kettle black." He's inviting us into an adventure while we're satisfied sitting in the library. He's demonstrating how He gives total access to someone as fallible as me and asking me to emulate that in the world around me. We'll never love people perfectly, but we can try to do it exhaustively, persistently, and honorably. If you're willing to live in the tension of building healthy boundaries to protect your joy and purpose while letting a few people in, here are some tips I've picked up along the way from the stories I have told you.

First, hearing your name called out doesn't always mean God has sent someone your way. Some people are just distractions to you. It's not lost on me that Twitter Dude called my name but wasn't the one I was planning to see. We sometimes confuse random conversations with divine appointments, and divine directives with questionable suggestions. Jesus said sheep know what the Shepherd's voice sounds like. The more experiences we have and the more we understand what the Scriptures say, the more easily we can distinguish Jesus' voice from the voice of some guy in a Suburban.

Second, just because we have an opportunity to do something

doesn't mean it's what God has in mind for us. Everyone wants to do whatever God wants them to do. I haven't met many people who disagree with this part. The problem is when people describe God's "plan" like it's a secret map in His back pocket He won't let us see. Or they peg some random event like a branch falling as a sign from above, which in one sense it kind of is. Could He communicate to us this way? Of course. He could hit you with the whole tree if He wanted to get your attention. But He could also write it down and hand it to you, and He has—if you will take the time to read what is already there in His love letters to us.

Third, anyone who stands at our door and knocks isn't necessarily Jesus. Lots of people will tell you they think God told them to tell you to do something. That's fine, I suppose, but the best way to make sure it's Jesus talking is to read what He's already said. God's commands are usually not confusing. We've only got two things to decide, really. First, how do these things God has said apply to me? And second, am I willing to do them?

Being stalked is a pretty obvious distraction and a joy killer. Be careful and discerning about who you let in and give pieces of yourself to. Stalking Jesus is a little more difficult to spot because it *seems* like we are doing the right things when we're actually doing little to nothing at all. Don't let the stalkers distract you while they are sorting things out in their lives—and don't forgo sorting out your own stuff and getting into a real relationship with Jesus.

CHAPTER 9

TOOTH FAIRIES AND SHRINKING AIRPLANES

Doubt is a powerful invitation when you trust God is big enough to allow your disbelief.

Several years ago there was an episode of *This American Life* on NPR that caught my attention.[1] The whole episode is dedicated to childhood misunderstandings that become actual beliefs. Let me give you a couple of examples from the show.

There was a young girl around four years old at the airport. She had seen planes before from the ground, but this was her first flight. Once airborne, the little girl turned to her seatmate and asked, "When do we get smaller?" You see, in her mind, she always saw airplanes as tiny floating toys from her perspective on the ground. It was actually quite brave of her to get on a plane thinking she was going to shrink when she took to the sky.

Another girl named Rebecca recalled a childhood friend who

lost a tooth. Rebecca's friend was pretending to be asleep when her dad came in, took the tooth, and slipped some money under the pillow. The next day, the friend told Rebecca, "I know who the tooth fairy is."

"Really! Who?" Rebecca replied, aghast.

"It's my dad," said the friend.

Rebecca could hardly believe it. Here's what she recounted on the episode: "I remember running home after school and telling my mom, 'Mom, I know who the tooth fairy is!' . . . And [the mom] said, 'Really? Who is the tooth fairy?' And I said, 'Rachel's dad is the tooth fairy! Ronnie Loberfeld is the tooth fairy!' And she said, 'I can't believe you know. It's totally secret. You can't let anyone else know. But you're right, Ronnie is the tooth fairy.'"

Cute stories like this make us chuckle. But guess how long one kid believed airplanes shrink and the other thought that Ronnie Loberfeld is the tooth fairy? Years and years. You and I have more than a few things we have believed. Some are true and others aren't, and it will take a lifetime to figure out which pile they go in.

Not all our beliefs are facts, and not all facts end up rising to the level of belief either. Sometimes our beliefs are sticky bits of hearsay that seem true but in fact are absolutely false. Most times, this won't cause us much harm. But when it comes to our faith, false beliefs can become distractions that have the power to rob us of a lifetime of clarity and purpose. Sometimes we need to figure out the truth about what we believe, meaning many of the cute explanations and assumptions we've grown familiar with might need to be revisited.

Take one of your early beliefs. You pick it. Broken mirrors? Black cats? Santa Claus? Heaven? If we have the courage to slide these beliefs under the microscope, we may find some misguided motivations for why we accepted them so readily. Maybe we wanted to tuck some happy thoughts into our pockets. Or maybe we wanted acceptance from a group or to remove the discomfort of uncertainty. These adopted beliefs felt like safe harbors at one time, but now they have us feeling trapped. Maybe we don't want to rock the boat with questions, so we end up failing to rock our lives by looking for the real answers. Here's the crazy part: This avoidance strategy works, or at least it seems to.

Countless people have joined a club of like-minded others who behave in a certain way instead of actually finding, understanding, and believing what is true. This is one of life's most grand and soothing distractions. If we're not careful, we can trade what could have been a meaningful, joyful, purposeful, and fully engaged life for fitting in, being accepted, or feeling like we are part of the crew. My question to you is this: If your faith is important to you, are you seeking a genuine expression of it or simply admittance to a club? If we want to live intentional lives, we need to decide *for ourselves* what we really do believe. We have to leave behind the assumptions we've made about what we ought to believe, as well as the facts we have ignored and the mistruths we've borrowed from someone else just to belong somewhere. One of the enduring beauties of the message that Jesus came in person to deliver can be summarized in these two words: *You belong.*

It can be a scary leap. I get it. But would you rather believe that airplanes shrink? A more beautiful truth exists. Be honest and authentic as you do this important work for yourself. Remember, Jesus never had a problem with people who were uncertain. He actually chastised the people who feigned absolute certainty for the bump of power and prestige they thought their knowledge would earn them. I'll be vulnerable here and give an example from my life.

I believe to my core that heaven exists. The Bible as well as my own instincts tell me this, but sometimes I wonder why I have concluded it is for real. It's a hope informed by my belief that the

Bible is true and how Jesus spoke of it with certainty. But this belief is not informed by my experience. While I have heard stories about people making the round trip there, I haven't been to heaven and I don't know anyone who went and came back. I don't know about you, but I'm just not wired to hear or read something and accept it wholesale. I know God isn't mad at me for that piece of who I am, but it nevertheless causes doubts. The only way this doubt can be resolved is for me to actually die, so it's a trade-off that isn't on my to-do list right now.

Now, some of you might be squirming in your seat with this kind of discussion, especially if you think people who write books, stand in pulpits, or sit in pews should have everything figured out. If this is you, it might do you some good, and it would certainly be good for the people around you, if you could chill out. If you were raised in a faith community that shakes its head and wags a bony finger at this kind of honest discussion, I say this with all the love and respect I can muster: Try to dial that back a little bit, okay? Get a puppy if you need to. We don't need this kind of distraction in our faith communities and in our lives. What we need is a fully vetted and honest set of beliefs born out of safe and honest conversations and informed by a close reading of the Scriptures. Doubt, done well, can lead to immense clarity and purpose. Try not to distract other people with an invitation to join your club when they are genuinely searching for truth, which can be hard-earned but has a much longer shelf life. Bring all your questions to Jesus. He can handle it.

There was a man who came to Jesus and, in a moment of raw authenticity and clarity, said, "I do believe; help me overcome my unbelief."[2] Wait, what? I believe and I don't believe at the same time? How could this be? It's simple. We all have doubts. Some people do the brave work of understanding their faith, and others ignore or defer the questioning. If you've got things about your faith you can't get your head around, don't fake it and act like you are certain. Please don't camp out in confusion by shrugging your shoulders and walking away from the thoughts and questions. Instead, get real with the questions and doubts you have. Stop pretending you don't have any; rather, bring them to Jesus and ask for His help in sorting them out. This will take more than a dollop of time, introspection, and honesty, but it will give God something authentic of yours to work with—perhaps for the first time.

Faith is simple, but it's not easy. The Bible describes faith as "confidence in what we hope for and assurance about what we do not see."[3] I like that description. We need to do more than just decide who our faith is in. We need to decide what our faith is actually about. I'll give you an example.

When my sons were in high school, I hoped one day they would graduate. Some days it felt like a fifty-fifty chance because they were interested in so many things, and school wasn't always one of them. Nevertheless, I still hoped. I also didn't see much homework coming home. If their reporting was accurate, no homework had been assigned—for all four years of high school. *Really?* It sounded suspect to me. Still, I kept the faith. Taking a cue from the Bible, I had confidence in what I was hoping for (graduation), and I had assurance in what I had not seen (homework). You can too.

What are you hoping for? Are you impatient for that thing to arrive or happen? Me too. What haven't you seen yet? Is it a job? A break? A relationship? A much-needed bailout? Can you trust that it might happen soon, even though it hasn't yet? This is what Jesus said real faith looked like. It wasn't having all the answers, though some would have you believe faith is unwavering confidence in your knowledge. Instead, faith is having the guts to ask the questions about your beliefs, knowing God's love is big and patient enough to cradle us in our unbeliefs.

Faith is also having the guts to actually do something about what you say you believe.

Several years ago there was this incredibly hot day, which is pretty unusual for where I live in San Diego. Waves of heat were rising off the pavement, and no one was outside. You could feel the lethargy overtaking the city because of the oppressive heat. It was like we were one big dog sleeping in the shade with his tongue sticking out, trying to cool down. To beat the heat, I called up my son Adam to see if he wanted to join me for some swimming out in the ocean. We loaded up the boat and left the bay heading west. These are the moments when I wish I had a trident or a swashbuckling hat or at least a sword and a pirate flag. I love going out into the open sea with the wind in my face and the boat's prow cutting through the chop.

Once we were far enough out to sea, we stopped the engines. Adam and I looked at each other and each did cannonballs into the water. The instant we hit the cool Pacific, the exact refreshment we needed engulfed us. We dove deep, splashed each other, and looked through the blurry water for fish and whales and mermaids. Adam swam back to the boat and I stayed in the cool water for a while longer, floating on my back with my eyes closed and allowing myself to become lost in the simple beauty of the moment. When I looked up, I noticed that the wind was pushing the boat away from me faster than I could swim back to it. It was like I had become part of a scene from the movie *Cast Away*, but I was the volleyball named Wilson.

If you've ever been in this kind of situation, it can feel a little scary—yet we have all experienced some version of this emotion. It may not have involved a boat drifting away from you, but rather a relationship or a hope or a business opportunity or a dream. Granted, I had Adam with me, so I knew I wasn't alone trying to get back to the boat. But the situation gave me a taste of fear and isolation and urgency, and it reminded me of that famous moment from the Bible when Jesus invited Peter to step out of the boat and join Him out on the waves.[4]

Jesus had just finished feeding thousands of people by making something out of nothing.[5] A little later, the disciples pushed away from shore in their boat going ahead of Jesus. Halfway across the sea, cue the big waves and wind. Maybe the disciples were scared just like I was when I couldn't get back to my boat. They had already endured one storm with Jesus where they thought the end had come for them.[6]

God will whisper to us in our comfort and shout to us in our pain.[7] Seemingly out of nowhere, Jesus showed up—walking on the water, no less—and gave Peter the chance not only to believe his faith but also to *show* his faith through his actions. It is an invitation we get every day. You might remember how the story goes. Peter volleyed into the wind and the waves: "Lord, if it's you . . . tell me to come to you on the water." I'm not sure who else Peter thought it might be. His landlord? One of his creditors? His father-in-law? The Domino's guy with a falafel pizza? Jesus didn't make a big speech or a three-point sermon. He just said, "Come," and with this one word all the water in the Sea of Galilee shifted to Peter's side of the tub. This happens to all of us at some point and in many different ways. God is not in the business of mansplaining His position; His style is to offer us simple invitations that will change the courses of our lives if we take Him up on the offers. "Come." He doesn't want us to agree with Him; He wants us to do something about our beliefs and engage the world.

You know the rest of the story. Peter got out of the boat and walked on the water in the direction of Jesus. I can guess Peter was a little more than tentative as he found his footing. Imagine the different camera angles for a moment. Peter was asking Jesus for His ID when he said "if it's you." I bet Jesus saw a guy who was curious and cautious. Peter's friends in the boat saw a guy doing the impossible. I can imagine the fish were totally freaking out and elbowing each other with their fins at the spectacle unfolding overhead.

When we take a big risk with our faith, distractions seem the most ready to derail us. This is what happened to Peter. He didn't find a soft spot in the water that caused him to sink; he got distracted by the wind and the waves and it punched a hole big enough to sink his journey toward Jesus. Here's my question for you: What is distracting you? Is it your work? Half of my friends are afraid they'll lose their jobs, and the other half are afraid they will keep them. Is it a difficult relationship? Maybe it's something in your past you are ashamed of or something in your future you are afraid of. Don't get punked by these things, and don't ignore them. Deal with them.

The first time Peter called out to Jesus from the boat, he asked Jesus to prove His identity. The second time Peter called out, he'd already seen the proof but realized upon sinking that he needed a boatload of help. If you have some doubts in your faith, it's not just okay; it's better than okay. Me too. Don't shrink back. Lean in. Take the risk and step out. But don't forget to call out to Jesus if you start to sink.

I took up a new sport a few years ago. It is overly generous to call what I was doing wakeboarding. I was mostly falling or dragging with a wakeboard attached to my feet. From the shore it probably looked more like trolling for big fish with me as the large piece of old, freckled bait. As I neared the boat after another failed attempt at getting up, I held out my hand to a friend who'd walked to the back of the boat to help pull me up and out of the water. I reached up intending to grab his hand like a handshake. Instead, my friend grabbed me wrist-to-wrist and reminded me this is how God holds us. "Bob, even if you let go, I won't. I've got you" were his reassuring words.

Back to the story about Peter. Here's something the text doesn't highlight but I think is important: How did Peter get back to the boat? Don't miss this. God often does as much on the way back from our failures as He does on the way there with our aspirations. That night, Peter didn't walk on water once; he walked on it twice. After he sank, Jesus didn't toss Peter a pair of floaties or make him swim back to the boat. Instead He stretched out His hand and pulled him up. I'll bet you anything Jesus grabbed him wrist-to-wrist and said, "I've got you and won't let go even if you do."

God is still in the business of rescuing us from the waves. In Peter's moment of doubt, Jesus moved toward him, not away. Do the same and move toward Jesus. Here's why. Jesus engaged with Peter; He didn't shame him. Jesus' only question to Peter makes sense to me. He asked, "Why did you doubt?" Peter had just seen the miracle of feeding thousands that very day. He had seen people healed and even raised from the dead. It's tempting to think we would have behaved better, but would we? Do we?

Peter expressed his faith in two different ways that night. The first was a tentative request to join Jesus on the water. I can relate to what it feels like to pose an uncertain question, and I hope you will find the courage to ask Jesus a couple of your own. The second was an even more courageous admission by Peter: that he was sinking and needed to be rescued. And in this moment, we see the two sides of the faith coin: action and doubt. When you believe something so fully, you're willing to take a risk; and when you doubt something so genuinely, you're willing to cry out for help. Do these things, and you'll be on the right track. Saying we have faith without any doubt ignores our humanity and cheapens our faith rather than deepening it.

Don't ever think that God looks at your honest attempt to join Him with some uncertainty as a failure. He is ecstatic about every move you make toward Him, and He's ready to grip your wrist hoping you will grab His the moment you doubt the miracle He is up to in your life. Even if you let go of Him, He won't let go of you.

———

One of the hardest times to exert unshakable, undistracted faith is when someone we love is hurting and in pain. I've lost many people close to me to illness. Perhaps you have joined the ranks of those who have lost someone in the arc of life. In the last few years it seems as though loss is more pronounced and front-and-center than any other time I can remember. It's heartbreaking, but here's my question: How does faith respond to loss? Is it with doubt and thrashing and accusation? Is it with prolonged grief and bitterness? God certainly allows for all of these reactions when our faith is tested by loss. But I also think that loss, like doubt, is an invitation to step out courageously toward Jesus. However it is you experience setbacks or sadness, do so with intention.

I have a friend named Bill who received a difficult cancer diagnosis. Bill and his wife, Laurie, had an upcoming appointment regarding the treatments and regimen Bill would experience in the coming months to try and beat the disease. I flew down to Houston to be with my friends when the appointment date came.

Jesus had a brother named James who wrote a letter to young followers in his day. He talked about how they should help people when they were sick, saying they should put oil on their sick friends' heads.[8] I don't know how you grew up and how you expressed your faith, if at all, but the whole anointing-with-oil thing is way outside of my experience. It sounded like something ridiculous or mystical or at least messy, but I wondered as I flew to Texas why it wouldn't still apply.

In the Old Testament, oil was put on someone's head in ceremonies to set that person apart or set them up for something big. They did it to kings and other important people about to do courageous things. James didn't say what would happen if you anointed someone with oil, and I think that's the point. Obeying what God invites us to do even before we understand it is an act of faith that God honors. When I tell God I want to have it all explained to me before I will obey, it makes faith sound like a negotiation—and it's not.

When I landed I decided to get some oil for Bill's head. I was a little unsure what kind of oil I needed. Extra virgin olive? Castor? Coconut or vegetable? I ruled out SAE 30 and crude because it didn't seem to fit even though we were in Texas. I figured I could find a grocery store on the way to the hospital. Unfortunately, I discovered there weren't any stores on my route, and I was pressed for time. But get this: There *was* a Burger King. I went inside, explained my dilemma to the guy at the fry machine, and talked him out of a cup of used oil from the deep fryer.

I turned more than a few heads as I walked through the hallways at MD Anderson with my cup full of oil that afternoon. I looked like a guy in a hurry carrying around his own urine sample. When I found Bill and Laurie, they were waiting for more tests. We prayed together that they would have the courage and clarity and undistracted focus to fight this battle and that the doctors would have extra wisdom to know what to do next. When we were done, I dipped my finger into the oil and then touched Bill's forehead. I'm sure he was the only guy who went into the MRI machine that afternoon smelling like a bag of french fries. Bill and Laurie are beacons of courage and joy, and Jesus and I have figured out why. They live undistracted lives.

A diagnosis like Bill's can bring one's life into laser focus. When you think about it, we all have a date with our mortality; we just don't know when it will be. If we can get our minds around this inevitability, things that once distracted us might no longer have a hold on us. Faith that once seemed unshakable might need to find new footing. This isn't just understandable. It is right-minded.

We have an opportunity every day to courageously make room for our doubts and embrace Jesus in the midst of them. We can step out and risk showing our faith—and cry out for rescue when we fail. The alternative is to remain distracted and afraid. The worst thing we can do is grip our familiar but outmoded beliefs and assumptions and claim them as truth. If we do, when we need them most, wobbly, untrue beliefs will have us looking for tooth fairies and shrinking airplanes. Bold faith is meant to work in the real world, but it requires that you and I first become real in our faith. Reach out your hand if you are in need. Don't try to shake hands with Jesus like you are closing a business deal; let Him grab you wrist-to-wrist.

CHAPTER 10

COUNT YOURSELF
AMONG THE STARS

*Availability can launch more dreams
than you could ever imagine.*

When I was in college, I wrote a letter to a popular musician from Texas named Keith Green. A few days later, I received a letter back from him. It probably would have seemed like a small thing to anyone else, but it wasn't to me. I opened his letter, and it only had three handwritten sentences. I don't even remember what the words were, but it doesn't matter. Those three simple sentences from a person I looked up to told me I mattered. They made me feel valued and let me know I was worth his time. I felt seen.

We all want the same things in life: love, acceptance, and connection. I wasn't a person trying to monopolize Keith Green's time, and I wasn't important by any standard the world measures. I knew who he was, but he had certainly never heard of me. I think I know what happened. I bet he received my letter and assumed that I was a young guy, thirsty for the same things everyone else wants. He didn't give me what he had the most of, which was advice; he gave me what he had the least of, which was his time. It was a cool cup of water on a hot day, and it is my earliest memory of feeling a profound sense of gratefulness for the gift of having been acknowledged by a stranger. He didn't hold on to his love like it was in short supply; he gave it away freely like he was made of it. He showed me that when it comes to generous acts of selfless love, we are rivers, not reservoirs.

Keith Green passed a few years later in a tragic airplane accident, but the few intentional moments of his life he gave to me blossomed into a pattern that has changed the way I connect with people who reach out to me. Gratefulness isn't just a feeling we hang on to like a dusty high school trophy; it's a response we pass along like a breeze. Each of us is a conduit of love. We don't need to fire off a thousand fireworks to express our gratitude; sometimes lighting one candle will do. We have the ability to shape and transform one another through the smallest acts of kindness and attention. The reason is simple. God doesn't pass us messages; He gives us each other. Sometimes three simple sentences are enough to change the entire trajectory of your life and someone else's.

———

When it comes to availability, there are three main ways we can create it: our time, our talent, and our treasure. Time and talent are self-defining and sometimes easier to understand than to give away. By "treasure" I mean our money, and I think this is worth hovering over for a moment if we are going to live undistracted and joy-filled lives.

When I wrote my first book, *Love Does*, it started as a dream to capture some of my life experiences to give to my kids. Then my friends Don and Bryan made themselves available to me, and it became a *New York Times* bestseller instead. They contributed their time and talents to make the book worth reading, and my kids promised me they would read the book if I wrote it—so I figured all the time spent trying to fix typos would be worth it.

We decided to use the proceeds of the book's sales to build schools and safe houses in Somalia, Iraq, Uganda, the Democratic Republic of Congo, Afghanistan, and a few other countries where long-standing civil wars had robbed kids of opportunities to learn and grow in safe, caring environments. After my friends made themselves available to me, quite a few more people gave up a little of their treasure to buy the book. This paved the way for almost a hundred buildings to sprout up into schools around the world, which created opportunities for thousands of kids to learn each year. Just a little bit of availability from a few kind friends led to *all of that*. If you happened to buy my first book, *you* played a part in all of this too. You created a giving community to serve needy communities. High fives and chest bumps all around.

When I put my cell phone number on the last page of that book, as well as every other book I have written, everyone thought I was crazy. I did it because thirty years earlier, a kind man had taken the time to write me three sentences. I get more than a hundred calls a week, and I don't send people to voicemail when I am in cell range. Every time I answer the phone and say hello, it's like I've told the person calling that they matter, they're valued, and they're worth my time. That's how I know I'm living an undistracted life: when I'm joyfully, abundantly, and unreasonably available to the people around me. I am certain that to almost everyone else I look incredibly distracted when I am saying hello to strangers on the phone, but nothing could be further from the truth. What can appear like distraction from afar can actually be wildly clear-eyed purpose, focus, and joy on display. I take calls in the elevator (mainly to break the awkward silence). I take calls in the courtroom. I've taken calls on stage while speaking to thousands of people, waiting in line at the DMV, at Disneyland, in the grocery store, on the way up Mount Kilimanjaro, and just about any other place you can imagine. Except the bathroom. Sorry if that was you calling, but I just won't. There are some things you can't unhear.

My purpose means staying incredibly available to people, but please hear me when I say this: This is *not* how life has to look for you if you aren't wired this way. I've already told you, even I have boundaries in this department. Like I've said, we are meant to be *one,* not the *same.* Your undistracted, wildly purposeful life may demand you throw your phone into the ocean so you can get back to the things you are meant to do. If that's the case and you need to throw your phone away, just give me yours because mine is old, beat-up, and cracked. Think of it this way. Getting rid of a big distraction has everything to do with being available elsewhere, right?

Maybe your thing is ridding yourself of distraction so you can dial up your availability and presence with things that matter way more than Netflix. None of us knows when our time here will end, but I think I know what my last minute or two will be like. I think that moment will be filled with tremendous gratefulness for the people I made time for and who made time for me. This is in large part why I want to make myself available to others. It is why I write books, take calls, and sit at Tom Sawyer Island at Disneyland on Wednesdays. Perhaps you're asking yourself, *Why be available at all?* Well, because Jesus was, for starters. Being available doesn't make us Jesus; it just makes us a tiny bit more like Him, and anything that nudges me more in His direction, I'm willing to do. If being available isn't for you, don't feel bad. If it's not your thing, love and embrace this about yourself. Just don't complain about not being pursued by others. Perhaps they are wired the same way.

Doing things that matter doesn't mean just doing things that are easy. Some of the ideas in this book will no doubt be hard for you to implement. I get it. These things are hard for me to put wheels on too. Try it anyway, even if it's hard. When Jesus was in the garden of Gethsemane, He uttered two sentences: "If it is possible, may this cup be taken from me. Yet not as I will, but as You will."[1] He didn't try to control the outcome, even when He knew it would be painful. Later, when Jesus was on the cross, He said, "It is finished" as He died and destroyed death.[2] In that moment, He created a pathway to love for us; He made God available to us through His sacrifice and presence. He did hard things in life—as well as the hardest thing One could do—and He hopes we will do the hard things too. His entire purpose was three sentences long.

———

Northern Uganda is home to the Acholi people, and it is ground zero for Uganda's most recent civil war. As is the case with most civil wars, everyone in the country lost. The Acholi people probably lost the most. Of the lives the civil war didn't take, the HIV virus took many. More than 1.7 million people were displaced, and when I first arrived, a thousand people were dying every week in makeshift camps. As a result of this perfect storm of tragedy, the average age of the entire country was reduced to just over fifteen years old.

We started a school in the area where the greatest number of child abductions took place. Most of the pioneer children we admitted to our school had been soldiers or were orphaned by the civil war or disease. They all needed new families, so we divided the hundreds of kids into family groups, and each family was led by one of the teachers.

For the first few years, we rented some small buildings for our school. But we quickly outgrew them, so we found a fifty-acre plot of land in a remote place in the bush in Northern Uganda and bought it. Coming from our humble digs, we felt like we had just purchased Texas. The country lacked the legal infrastructure to even grant land titles to anyone's land, so we formed a land board in our region and began giving property deeds. Ours was the first.

We dug wells, built roads, swept the land for unexploded ordnance, and started building a school for the kids. We have been busy since then. There are now sixty buildings; five wells; thirty teachers; computer, physics, and chemistry laboratories; a regulation soccer field (or football pitch, depending on where in the world you're reading this); and more than sixteen hundred students who show up every day. Most of them live on campus in the dorms we—you—built. The Republic of Uganda only has two Olympic-size tracks in the country. We have one of them. We are also the highest taxpayer in the entire region—a distinction I'm not particularly excited to claim. I guess what I'm telling you is that *we—you and I and the others—all built a city together.* All we need is a post office and a fire department. Check in with me in a year, and I bet we will have those too.

I have so many stories to tell about the school, but one that could stop me in my tracks is about a student named Obomo. He was twelve years old when we met. His parents had been dragged from their hut by rebels with the Lord's Resistance Army and burned alive in front of him. I know that is hard to read, but that really happened to Obomo. His relatives didn't have a way to provide for him or to give him an education. When I heard Obomo's story, I knew exactly what to say: "You're in." I gave him a big bear hug, grabbed his young hand, and introduced him to his new family at the school.

He came to us lost, scared, and without hope. At first he felt like he didn't fit in. He was traumatized but resilient; he was trying to make sense of his life and the world around him as a young man. As time went by, Obomo grew in his academics and relationships at the school. He began taking on more leadership roles, and he was a joy to his teachers and an encourager to his peers. Even among a school full of diamonds, he shined bright. This upward trajectory lasted throughout all the years he was with us.

High school graduation day approached, and the students were popping with excitement. They had not only survived a war but had excelled in their education. I was in the school office printing diplomas that had a knockoff of Harvard's insignia. I know, I know. Sue me. One of my favorite moments in the history of the school was placing the valedictorian medal over Obomo's head. Do you have any doubt that Obomo will open doors of possibility to others through his availability? Of course you don't. Me neither. This is what availability does; it reminds us of our purpose and leads others to their purposes too. Availability spawns opportunity; opportunity inspires more availability; and the cycle carries on and creates deeper purpose.

———————

In Northern Uganda, the night sky is bright with stars. If you live in a major city, small town, or suburb, or near any houses or floodlights, you may not be able to fully visualize what I mean. In vast stretches of the African bush, there is almost zero light pollution. The night sky is riddled with glorious, sparkling pinpricks. Thousands upon thousands upon thousands of shards of light traveling expanses we cannot conceive. You can see a spiraling arm of the Milky Way stretching out past the horizon, and every falling star that streaks across the sky is a reminder of who God is and who we are not.

Uganda is not the kind of place that would have a space program. But since the time our students were young children, they have looked up to the sky from their villages with a kind of wonder the vastness stirs inside each of us. NASA stopped flying the space shuttle, and most of their funding was cut several years ago too. When I learned of this I called and asked if they had any spare parts we could have sent to our school in Gulu. A space capsule? A spare booster rocket? Really, anything would be nice. I imagined giving people directions to our school and telling them to "turn after the first rocket ship." Uganda had never launched anything into space. I looked at the GoPro camera on my desk and started to wonder: *What if our kids were the first?*

Since NASA was basically out of business, we decided to establish Gulu's first space program. We called it GASA. I knew every junior high school kid would love that, no matter where they lived. I found some tanks of helium in Mombasa, Kenya, and had them shipped to Gulu. It cost me more than four giraffes. We enlisted an astronaut from NASA, the owner of an airline, and some others to help us with the caper, and we got to work.

A few months later we traveled to Gulu. Once there my son Rich put a GoPro camera wrapped with hand warmers in a Styrofoam ice chest. Then we began filling a weather balloon with helium. It inflated to fifteen feet across and twenty feet high. The students counted down and let go. A thousand sets of eyes watched as it soared into the air. The students nominated their own flight control captain. When the balloon was off the ground, she yelled, "We have liftoff! Look at it go! Where will it land?" Three more sentences.

Children who were once handed Kalashnikov rifles were now cheering and crying and hugging as they all became part of Uganda's first space launch. They had a new family—a bright future—and they could soar as high as their imaginations would allow them. But this launch wasn't just a metaphor; we still had a school to run and lessons to teach. With the help of a friend who understood meteorology, the kids calculated how the winds aloft would influence the trajectory of the balloon, then predicted in their physics class calculations where the balloon would end up.

Rich had put a GPS in the ice chest so we could monitor the balloon after the launch. Every three minutes we got a new ping. The students tracked the balloon as it drifted south over the country and climbed to over one hundred thousand feet. It entered the edge of space, and by the time it reached this elevation, it grew even bigger as the atmosphere thinned. It's like when you fill a water balloon too full but keep going, knowing it's going to pop any second. That's what this moment was like but with fewer swimsuits. And then it happened. The vacuum of space popped the balloon, and the remnants began their descent to earth. Rich had also attached a parachute to the ice chest, and the kids huddled around the computer as we tracked its progress back to Uganda. The package was right on course with where the students had predicted it would land.

Suddenly the wind shifted. Students scrambled to calculate new trajectories, running about waving their arms. Team leaders shouted across the room. There was a tremendous amount of energy and focus as these young people sized up the task before them. It was awesome. I felt like I was in Houston during Apollo 13, but there was no red phone to say "we have a problem." The kids figured out the new trajectory, and as it turned out, the payload decided to drift more than one hundred miles to the west. The new landing zone we triangulated was in a different country, the Democratic Republic of Congo (DRC). Not good.

Once the package touched ground, we could see from a satellite image exactly where the GPS had located the camera. There were six small grass huts one hundred yards away, and we assumed the box had landed in a field or was snagged in the thick jungle canopy. Every three minutes we continued to receive a new fix on our Styrofoam box, but within an hour, something changed. The GPS indicated the box was now inside one of the huts. A few minutes later, it was in another hut. Within the hour, it had gone to all the huts. I can only imagine what the villagers must have been thinking as they carried the box with the parachute and camera that had been in space from hut to hut. Kind of like a movie.

One of the guards at the school is named Cosmos. I'm not kidding. I'm so disappointed that my parents picked the name Bob for me. Cosmos is from a village in the DRC near where the box landed, so we sent him over the border to see if he could get it back. A few hours later, Cosmos called to inform us that he had figured out exactly where the box and GoPro camera were.

The next call we got was from the DRC's military. Cosmos had been arrested as a spy. Yikes! The military saw the box, the camera, and the parachute and got understandably ruffled by it. Suddenly, this mission had gone as horribly sideways as the parachute had. So we called some friends in Uganda who called some generals in Uganda who called some generals in the DRC, and Cosmos was released that same night. Talk about a misunderstanding. We got the camera back, but they took the flash drive so we couldn't replay the descent from the edge of space. I still have my request in to the government for it.

Here's my point. Not everything went exactly as we planned, but who cares, right? A couple of things will go right for you, and a couple simply won't. God doesn't keep score, and you shouldn't either. When we are tempted to bring Him only our successes, God reminds us He delights at our attempts even when they fail. The kids still talk about their space mission. That's what a little bit of availability and a lot of helium will do. "We have liftoff!

Look at it go! Where will it land?" What will your next courageous move be?

Since graduating from our school in northern Uganda, Obomo
applied to law school three times and was denied each time. He was
at the top of the class at our school, but still, there are only a couple
of law schools in Uganda, and competition for the few available
spots is fierce. The first time he told me he wanted to be a lawyer
was when he'd arrived at our school more than a decade earlier. He
had seen firsthand what injustice looked like and wanted to be part
of the solution for his country. This passion to be a lawyer never left
him, and we talked about it often throughout his years of primary
and high school. We joked about opening up a law firm together
called "Obomo & Bob." Kind of a catchy name, I thought.

After graduation, his dream of being a lawyer seemed both near
and far away. He called me shortly after the first time he had been
turned down for law school. I told him to go sit on the dean's bench
until they let him in. He thought I was kidding, but this was a tactic
I employed in my own life, so I was certain it would improve his
chances. (If you've read *Love Does*, you know what I'm talking
about.)

Obomo called me the second time he was turned down, and I
told him to go back and sit on the dean's bench again. "This time,"
I told him, "don't leave until they let you in." I bet he thought I was
still kidding, but instead of thinking about the unfairness of his
rejection and the steep nature of the mountain he was climbing, he
got tenacious. He went again, met with the dean, and told him again
why he wanted to get in. He spoke about losing his parents and
finding the school. He spoke about his dedication and commitment

to his classes. He told him about his dream to bring more justice to Uganda.

Then he asked the dean if he had ever launched anything into space. When the dean said no, Obomo told him that if he helped him become a lawyer, it would be considered an even bigger launch than the one he and his classmates had completed. The dean gave a long pause, shuffled some papers around on his desk, looked up, and said to Obomo: "You're in." It wasn't the first time Obomo had heard these words.

What has got you distracted? What is the big ambition you've been trying to launch that seems to be stuck on the tarmac? I know it's hard; much of life is hard. Get back at it. Keep showing up for yourself and the people who will benefit if you don't quit. You are probably just a few sentences away from the next grand adventure. Find a couple of people who will make themselves available to you. Be the kind of person who will be available to others, and start pointing toward the stars once again with awe and wonder and undistracted and relentless determination. Start the countdown. The angels in heaven are itching to look at your life and say, "We have liftoff! Look at you go! Where will you land?"

CHAPTER 11

"CEASE FIRE!"

The words we use can become weapons
or heal wounds. Choose wisely.

Where we live in San Diego backs up to a bay with a marina. Oftentimes we sit on our back porch and watch the languid boat traffic come in and out of the harbor. There are dinghies and pontoon boats, skiffs and sailboats, paddleboarders, Jet Skis, and kayakers. One day when the kids were in high school, they came home and announced they had each been given an assignment to write an essay on any topic they wanted. It was one of those almost perfect days when it seemed the whole world wanted to play hooky and be outside. Joggers were on the paths, dogs were catching Frisbees, picnickers were napping on their blankets, and anything that floated was coming and going. The kids gazed out the back window to the world they wished they could join and glanced down dejectedly at empty pages needing to be filled with good stories.

After a snack and some muffled grumbling about their

homework, they all trudged upstairs to their bedrooms. They each had a desk against a window that happened to face—you guessed it—the water. After an hour passed, I ducked into their rooms to see how things were going. Each of the kids seemed to be in a trance, daydreaming and gazing out the windows, making no progress on their assignments. Shortly after checking in, something started coming into view on the water from around the bend to the north. It was an old-school square-rigged sailing ship, like the kind the British Navy had back in the seventeenth century. It had cannons and loads of sails of various sizes. I got out my binoculars to see if they had a plank, too, and were going to make someone walk it.

Because I had just seen the kids gazing out their windows, I knew they were seeing this as well. It's not every day one of these pirate ships comes into the bay, and I knew the kids were looking for a distraction. Then it got even better. A few minutes later *another* tall ship came into view, just as large and grand and with as many sails and cannons as the first one.

The ships both started doing maneuvers and circling in the water like a dance, taking wide arcs and cutting into the wind. You could see the sea-foam crashing off the prows as the boats leaned into their turns. It dawned on me what we were witnessing: two tall ships about to roll their cannons out to enact a sea battle.

I ran upstairs and told the kids school was dismissed. They got so much air jumping out of their chairs they must have been spring-loaded. The afternoon had gotten a lot more interesting, and I hoped that if maybe we got in the mix, the day's events would inspire their school assignment they still needed to write when we got back. We quickly made our way to the water and jumped in our little family dinghy to get a closer look at the action. We considered drawing up plans to swing aboard on ropes and take command like pirates do, but we realized we had no ropes or masts to swing from. Plus, an aluminum painting ladder leaned up on the side from our dinghy lacked the swashbuckling vibe.

As we neared the battle, we decided the best view would actually be from *between* the ships. There would be enough space for our little boat, and we thought we could help one of the ships surrender if necessary or pick up anyone who fell overboard. The ships had finished their wide arcs and started to pass by each other in a parallel line with about fifty yards between them. I steered our boat right toward the middle of the action, and as soon as we were in position, small doors on both ships flipped open and cannon muzzles rolled out and forward. Then we covered our ears in anticipation of what was about to happen.

Deafening sounds exploded across the water as plumes of acrid smoke blasted out of each vessel in succession down the hull. These ships, of course, didn't shoot live cannonballs at each other but rather blanks that make a big bang. All told, between the two ships, they let off almost twenty cannon shots in the space of a few minutes until they were no longer in a line of sight to fire. We were left rocking back and forth in a cloud of smoke while we all whooped and hollered. We eventually made our way back to the house, and the kids ran upstairs to write their essays with a new story in mind. I'm pretty sure I put my fists on my hips and puffed out my chest a little for winning what I imagined should be the fun dad award for the afternoon.

The kids talked about this caper for days, which is why it was incredibly uncanny when we later heard a news report of a mock cannon battle in another harbor where one of the ships had accidentally shot *live fire* from their cannons. I don't mean they had cannonballs; these modern cannons used modified twelve-gauge shotgun shells to produce the blasting noise. One ship in the mock battle had somehow loaded both live and modified ammunition, having grabbed the wrong ammo boxes by mistake. Needless to say, they ruined the afternoon for some tourists. There were some injuries but nothing too serious, luckily.

It seems the world has been using a lot of live fire recently in our words with other people. Have you felt that? The words we have chosen have become mean-spirited and are laced with more hurtfulness, lies, and put-downs than I can remember being used before. I don't think people trying to make their points are always aware of the damage they are doing to other people's hearts or their own reputations, but the fact is, they *are* doing damage. When it comes to the words we use, we're never shooting blanks even though we think we are. In the Bible, Jesus said that our words are an overflow of whatever is in our hearts.[1] I agree and wonder if we understand that many of the words we are using have become distractions to ourselves and the people around us.

You have heard this saying before: "Holding on to anger is like drinking poison and hoping the other person dies." Take whatever negative emotion you are blasting at other people, and I think the metaphor equally and aptly applies. The words we use usually come straight from our hearts, and those words tend to show others what's happening beneath the surface in our lives. Do the words you use show a heart full of grace, love, and acceptance or one of disapproval, condemnation, and vitriol? Undistracted people go for a lot of the first batch and little to none of the second. Do your words invite pain or joy?

Don't get me wrong. No one here thinks life is always unicorns, daffodils, and rainbows. It is how we decide to receive and react to the hard parts of our circumstances that shows us what our hearts are filled with. I decided to put myself in the hot seat with my own words. I really wanted to know what was in my heart, so one year I decided to charge myself five hundred dollars a word for any criticism I uttered about anyone—no matter how right I thought I was or how badly I thought they deserved it. I picked that amount because it is about the cost of a plane ticket to Maui. Having this metric helped me decide whether I would rather go to Maui or say a sharp word about someone. It was a reminder to me that our words might be costing our relationships much more than most of us realize. It has been helpful to have my cutting, judgmental words cost me five hundred bucks a pop. These days, I try to only say the angry words I can afford to say, which isn't many.

After I spoke somewhere at a conference, some guys cornered me. I tried to step around them, but they blocked my path. They wanted to tell me how God doesn't love this group of people or that group of people based on their conduct and lifestyle. They were pretty animated as they gave me both barrels. I was in no mood for an expensive discussion, and I didn't have much I wanted to say to them. I just wanted to get home for supper with Sweet Maria. When I did try to say something, they interrupted me and got even more worked up. About the fifth time they interrupted me, I tried to walk away but they blocked my path. Unfortunately no one else was around to yell "Cease fire!" so I lit the fuse, let 'em have it, and said something I shouldn't have. On reflection, I got the anatomy right but the spirit of God wrong—and it cost me several plane tickets to Maui. Why? Simple. Because it became more important to me to be right than to be Jesus. I made it about me rather than about Him.

Let me give you an opposite example. In college, I attended a Bible study at a guy's home. His name was Brad, and he was the midpoint between my age and my parents' ages. He wanted to help college kids like me find their way forward. I was usually late arriving to Brad's Bible study because time was a fluid concept to me back then. If that frustrated Brad, he never let on. He would simply pause the group each week as I meekly ducked into the room and tried to find an open seat.

One week I happened to arrive a few minutes before we started. Brad pulled me aside afterward and said, "Bob, it really honors me that you are a guy who arrives on time." He wasn't trying to mess with my head or use reverse psychology on me; he wanted to speak into my heart. Looking back, I now realize what he was doing. He saw a better version of me that was within reach, and his words called it out of me. These weren't words of correction, they were words of affirmation. It's now forty years later, and guess what? I'm usually on time wherever I go. Do you know why? Because I was rude to a kind man named Brad who told me decades ago I was a guy who honored others by being on time. Our words have immense power to tear down or build up. Choose yours wisely with everyone. Don't distract others with negative scattershot. Your well-chosen words can shift the people around you toward something better and more beautiful instead.

———

There are places all over the world where real live fire is an everyday fact of life—along with the suppression of people whose voices need to be heard. The organization I started called Love Does is doing work in places like this because we want to help people find their hope and their voices again after being devastated by war or silenced by their gender or cultural traditions. One of the ways we do this is by opening schools for these young heroes and heroines, including girls' schools in countries where girls aren't usually taught to read.

Just outside of Mosul, Iraq, ISIS was buying and selling women and children in cages for twenty dollars apiece. Hearing what was happening to the Yazidi people appropriately angered the world.

There is a city outside the capital, Erbil, near the border of Iran, and with some terrific new friends in the region, we started a school and built housing for the Yazidi kids and their families who were displaced by ISIS. I was there when the building was complete and we welcomed our first student body. I remember walking into a classroom and giving a young Yazidi girl a medal, pinning it to her chest, and saying, "You are the hope of this country." I felt like I was Brad that day. We can actually speak that kind of courage and destiny over others, and the crazy part is, the people we do this to will become who we say they are.

Try it. If you are a parent, speak over your kids' lives the kind of beauty and hope their hearts long to hear. If you are a brother, sister, friend, priest, flight attendant, or zookeeper, find a few people close to you and speak words of truth and beauty over them too. Don't just agree with me. Go do this for somebody today. Do it for a firefighter or your mail delivery person or the attendant at the gas station. Find the person serving the food you eat or the one who picked it or is bagging it at the grocery store and tell them they are the hope of Detroit or Memphis or Lodi or wherever you are. It's likely they will find greater joy and purpose in what they do, and you will too.

God doesn't care where you are when you flood the zone with words of hope and joy and courage; He cares about who you are. This doesn't make you anyone's savior; it makes you a truth-giver, someone who can peer into someone's heart and call forth a part of its purpose. You're not blowing sunshine at people to tell them they are magnificent creations; you are seeing them the way God does. Can you imagine what would happen if we all did this with each other? Wouldn't the world be a better place? No longer would we be distracted by all the dark reasons and excuses we think have power over our circumstances. We would see that our lives are meant to be lived with tremendous impact and joy.

Because of the respect the local governor had for the people we were working with in Erbil, and the hope these kids in our school had, we were invited to meet with him. He is a fearsomely brave man and is widely known as the man who fired the first shot of the Iraqi Revolution. How cool is that? What do you give that guy? A vase? A flak jacket? A Slinky? I wasn't sure what to bring, so I brought him a balloon from San Diego. I'm not kidding. I had some kids blow it up with helium in the United States, then I carried it around the world to him. I told the flight attendant I had packed light as I put it into the overhead bin on the airplane, but I don't think she got it.

On the flight over, I also thought a lot about what I would say. Then I remembered, when it comes to Jesus, our job is to be love, not God's publicist or master of fancy words and spin. There's a reason we all know the phrases "actions speak louder than words" and "a picture is worth a thousand words." That balloon was probably the best speech I could give. The existence of that school was better than any commencement address I've given here in the United States. Don't get distracted thinking about what your next move is or whether you will be acknowledged for your efforts. Go love people in extravagant, wildly inefficient ways by speaking words of beauty into their lives. Your words have that kind of power. Get a couple in play and see what happens.

The autonomous region of Iraq in the north is called Kurdistan and is protected by courageous soldiers call the Peshmerga. This force's name literally means "those who face the death." ISIS had taken over the city of Mosul, and more than a million people were being held captive by them. The courageous Peshmerga soldiers had surrounded the city and were preparing to liberate it. We headed to the front line where the Peshmerga had dug into trenches. I was told to leave the balloon since it would be a really enticing target for the enemy. When we arrived, ISIS soldiers could be seen only a few hundred yards away, and soldiers on both sides intermittently exchanged fire. In addition to my balloon, I brought one more package with me filled with medals we had made. Once we reached the trenches, I pulled out my package of medals and went up and down the trenches pinning them on the chests of the soldiers. I let them know they, too, were the hope of the country.

It wasn't long before someone in charge of the entire operation came over and asked me who I was and what we were doing. He invited us back to the battle tent and asked if we wanted to see the plan for the liberation of Mosul. It was a fast yes for me and my friends. I was thinking they would have flat-screen monitors with satellite images, complicated communication channels, and complex maps with arrows and details inside. Instead, they had a six-by-eight-foot sandbox with plastic army soldiers in it. This was their plan. Honestly, I thought there would be more to it.

Here's God's plan for you and me. Our words can liberate the best in us. Don't overcomplicate it. Find words of love and affirmation and understanding that come from a heart liberated from cynicism and hatred. Search yourself. Are vestiges of these negative things lurking in the uncharted areas of your life? The more you hear beautiful, encouraging, life-giving words flowing out of your mouth, the more you know that is the person you're becoming too.

CHAPTER 12

THE WRONG BUTTON

Our failures don't mean that we are failures.

If you've never been to the Hawaiian Islands, you might not know they really are the stuff of legend. Palm fronds as big as kitchen tables drape over forest floors. Birds of paradise erupt out of the ground in plumes of neon orange and periwinkle. Ocean breezes dance over petrified lava flows black as charcoal. Waves crash on endless beaches and mosses descend even the steepest cliff faces. It seems like anything can grow there, and the people are as happy as you would expect them to be living in such a beautiful place.

Did you know that Hawaii became the fiftieth state in 1959? Seems pretty late in the game considering the United States was officially a country in 1776. To most of us, Hawaii is the definition of a dream vacation. It's not all grass skirts, coral reefs, umbrellaed drinks, and lounge chairs though. It is an archipelago of strategic national, geopolitical, and military importance too. Hawaii is America's doorway to the Asia-Pacific in the same way Alaska is

America's doorway to Russia. This is why Hawaii has eleven military bases representing all four major branches of the United States military and the coast guard. So Hawaii has some serious firepower too.

It was another beautiful day in Hawaii when a middle-aged man stepped through the doors of the Hawaii Emergency Management Agency. Looking at the outside of the building, you wouldn't expect anything impressive to be going on inside. Its low-lying, off-white double doors are the main entrance built into a small, brush-covered hillside. Behind those doors, however, something more exciting is afoot. Corridors go ever deeper and farther into the hillside, leading to rooms filled with screens and consoles covered in blinking lights, sensors, knobs, handles, and microphones. If you have ever heard of NORAD in Colorado, this place is basically the NORAD of Hawaii. As a country we had good reason for such a place. North Korea had launched missiles and developed a nuclear weapon, presumably for the purpose of leveling a place like this.

But back to that beautiful, normal day in Hawaii in January 2018. The man who walked through the double doors had made a huge mistake. A truly epic failure. He didn't scrape another car in the parking lot without reporting the accident or dine and dash at Denny's. Instead, during a training exercise to check the early warning systems for incoming intercontinental ballistic missiles, he got distracted and pushed the wrong button. When he did, he alerted all of Hawaii—and by extension the whole world—that the United States was under attack and should take immediate emergency action. The message that went through the Emergency Alert System and everyone's cell phones read as follows: "Incoming ballistic missile threat. This is not a drill." I'm sure you remember this event. It was a frightening moment for all of us, reminding those a few years ahead of a frosty day in Cuba amid the Cold War. We learned back then that one wrong button push could activate a cascade of bad decisions and end a lot of lives on all sides.

This is not a drill. I'm sure the national defense ministries were on the phone with each other. Friends and residents in Hawaii frantically called one another, and people on the islands stored food and water and headed for tunnels. People hid under bridges and hand-dug holes, while others said their goodbyes. I wouldn't be surprised if the president was ushered to the bunker below the White House.

After some scrambling and hubbub, reports were soon issued that the warning had been a huge mistake. Once the world collectively wiped its brow, everyone was furious. Some phrases come to mind that seem to inadequately capture the magnitude of the screwup. One wrong button pressed had massive implications for the entire planet and carried with it potentially dire consequences. Some failures are too severe to get a total pass, and the guy who pushed the wrong button got about as fired as a person can get. Everyone seemed okay with that under the circumstances. To protect his identity, news outlets and the Emergency Management Agency didn't release his name. But I figured out who he was and mailed him a letter. Inside the envelope was a job offer. I'm not kidding.

Why in the world did I make a job offer to this guy who had an epic fail? The guy who activated the facepalm to end all facepalms? Here's why: I did it because I didn't want him to think he was a failure just because he had failed. He had just been distracted. It happens to all of us, just in different ways. This is so important that I'll say it again: He was not a failure just because he had failed, and you aren't a failure just because you become distracted either. Dwell on this for a moment. If you have ever failed at something—and my guess is you have—your failure was an event, not your new identity. *You are not a failure because you screwed up.* A distraction that results in a failure doesn't mean you are any less beloved of God. Mistakes are reminders of our desperate need for Him in our lives.

Do you believe that? Can you believe that? The distracted people I've been talking about in this book know the difference between a failed attempt and being a failure as a person. How about you? Can you wrap your arms around the difference between the two? Figuring out this distinction will make all the difference in your life and in the lives of the people you interact with.

Why do we torture ourselves when things go wrong in big and small ways? Why do we aggregate all our little mess-ups and tuck them into the secret places of our hearts and the memory vaults in our minds for long-term storage? If you are like most people, I bet you remember way more mistakes you have made than your successes along the way. If you are like a lot of us, you have that harsh word or criticism you received from a teacher or ex-boyfriend or ex-girlfriend or boss or total stranger playing on repeat in your head. If we are to move forward captivated by immense purpose, we will have to learn a new way to process these unhelpful memories and move beyond our failed attempts.

I'm going to give you a few examples of people who failed miserably just to remind you that we are in good company when it looks like we have failed.

- Thomas Edison invented ten thousand ways not to have a light bulb before he successfully invented one.
- Bill Gates's first company failed miserably. It was called Traf-O-Data.
- Walt Disney was fired from a newspaper, citing his lack of creativity. His first company, Laugh-O-Gram, failed too. (To all you entrepreneurs reading this book, maybe don't name your company Dash-O-Dash.)

- Milton Hershey started three candy companies that didn't succeed before founding Hershey's Chocolate.
- Einstein couldn't speak fluidly until age nine, and he wasn't accepted as a student at Zurich Polytechnic School.
- In a Nike commercial from the late nineties, Michael Jordan said, "I've missed more than nine thousand shots in my career. I've lost almost three hundred games. Twenty-six times I've been trusted to take the game-winning shot and missed. I've failed over and over and over again in my life. And that is why I succeed."[1]
- J. K. Rowling lived in poverty as she spent seven years finishing the Harry Potter series, which was rejected by twelve publishers.

Okay, I know I went for the top shelf with these examples. Not everyone is going from epic fails to super successes, from rags to riches or starting world-shaping companies. Here's the thing though: If you believe you are a failure because you failed at something, you won't get to the things that matter. It's that simple. I have had some failures both personally and professionally. I've wrecked my airplane and a few relationships that were important to me. I have sunk a company and spent a few years putting my family in second place in my life because I thought I was providing for them without realizing I wasn't providing what they needed most, which was me. I lost my shirt once in a real estate deal in Washington DC, where I tried to help bring a little peace to the people in leadership but lost a boatload of money trying.

We all want our stories to be success stories, at least to some degree. We want to know that all our toil will eventually prevail. We want to be Rudy, running out onto the football field after years of noble efforts and making the big play. I love that we are wired this way. But have you ever experienced a total failure with no silver lining, no comeback story, no rising from the ashes? Some failures can't be undone, such as the Hawaii missile debacle. As humans we are wired to see the villain and the victim in these moments. I get it—I'm the same way. Massive hurt and brokenness can result from epic failures. But hear this: God still loves us. God loves the injured and the inmate. God rushes toward the prodigal and loves the faithful. I'm glad this is God's heart because His love for the undeserving is a reminder of His love for me, someone who is undeserving of it. That's the way He loves you and will always love you. I've said this before, and I'll say it again: Grace never seems fair until you need a little.

When our son Adam was an infant, we had a small house and were remodeling an upstairs room to be a bedroom. I was carrying Adam in my arms on the second floor and heard someone knock on the front door. As I turned the corner to go down the stairs, I stepped on the Wet Paint sign that had fallen to the floor on the first step. Both of my legs slipped out from underneath me. I went soaring, and it looked like I was going to be swan-diving down the entire flight of stairs.

You need to understand this all happened in half a second. Gravity works that fast. The instant I realized I was going to fall headfirst down the stairs with Adam in my arms, I instinctively reached my arms behind me and tucked him between the wall and the first stair as my trajectory aimed toward the first floor. Because I had put both arms behind me to hold Adam in place, I took the next twelve stairs right in the face like a bobsledder going down the track headfirst. I was a bruised, bloody, and battered mess, lying like a satchel of bones at the bottom of the stairs. We're talking Rocky Balboa when he lost to Ivan Drago. My eyes were closed and I groaned with pain as all my body parts checked in with me and told me how they loathed me. Meanwhile, Adam was unhurt—giggling and clapping as he was still tucked into the top stair.

Not unlike God protecting Moses in the cleft of a rock as He passed by. Or when I think about Jesus when He was on the cross, I see how a loving Father protects us. Jesus didn't splay His arms on the stairs like I did. Instead, He spread out His arms on a wooden cross. He was flung down into the depths for our sakes, and all the while He tucked us safely away until He had taken all the hits that were meant for us.

I worked for years on a legal case with plenty of financial upside at stake for my clients. When it was finally done, I packed up the family to go to Disneyland to celebrate. I was really looking forward to giving Mickey and Goofy some high fives.

Meanwhile, my co-counsel was on his way to close all the loops with our client after a long legal battle. He swung by the bank and picked up a cashier's check to give to the client. After he delivered the final paperwork and picked up the proceeds, he headed to the golf course. Golf isn't my thing, but my co-counsel loved to play and thought a round of golf would be the best way to commemorate finishing the case and getting back to a healthier pace of work. He put the cashier's check in his back pocket and hit the links.

On the ninth hole my co-counsel received a call on his cell phone from the bank; he was in his backswing and let it go to voicemail. On the twelfth hole he received another call on his cell phone from the bank; he was putting this time and let it go to voicemail. On the eighteenth hole he received a call on his cell phone from the bank; he was in the rough (again) and let it go to voicemail. After that, the calls came every two or three minutes. He finally picked up the phone. "What? What is it? What could possibly be so important that you would bug me all afternoon? Can't this wait until Monday?" He didn't even give the voice on the other end a chance to say anything. Turned out it was the president of the bank.

"Do you have the cashier's check we gave you?" the president asked.

"Sure, of course I do. It's in my wallet."

"Get out the check and take a look at it."

The cashier's check was supposed to be for one million dollars, a kingly sum by any measure. Except the check he held mistakenly had been made out for one *billion* dollars. That's right, billion with a *b*.

He dropped his club right where he stood and put his hand over his mouth. "What should I do?" he asked. "Ah, just keep it," the president said. And they all lived happily ever after.

Just kidding. This is exactly what didn't happen. My co-counsel was given precise instructions on how to return the cashier's check, which was as good as cash, promptly to the bank. Part of me wondered if snipers and helicopters and drones all had him under surveillance while he made his way back to the bank, but I was at Disneyland riding the Dumbo ride, so he was flying solo on this one.

What do you think your life is worth to God? A dollar? A million dollars? How about a billion dollars? To Him, there are not enough zeros to estimate the value of *you*. Here is the crazy promise of Jesus to us. When we fail miserably, spectacularly, epically, and when we become distracted by the less important things around us, the value of our stock with Him doesn't drop. You and I are still the apples of His eye and the pulse of His heartbeat. To Him you and I are eternally valuable; we all are.

There will be times in our lives when we push the wrong button at work, in a relationship, or amid an important decision or two. The inevitability of a mistake doesn't mean it is any less painful. It's time we stopped acting like our failures somehow disqualify us from God's love, when in reality these setbacks might lead to a keener awareness of it. The sacrifice Jesus made for us means that any failure we could ever conceive of is covered. He has taken it on the chin and in His hands and feet for us. When we stumble, He has us cradled in safety while we figure things out. We need to realize what we already have in our possession. Because of Jesus, we can know that our failures don't make us failures. They remind us we are His.

CHAPTER 13

PINOCCHIO'S NOSE

*We forego our purpose when we fake
it in our relationships to safeguard
a false feeling of safety.*

My friends and I were headed to the horse stables at our retreat center called The Oaks. Excited to share this new adventure with people I cared about, I took on the role of the host who wanted his guests to have a terrific time. I was pointing out my favorite parts of the property—the cows in the fields, the buildings we had remodeled over there, the waterslide, and the vineyard going in. I was acting like P. T. Barnum in complete control of the circus as we drove down to the barn. Inside, though, I knew the truth. I was a little nervous about getting on a horse because I actually knew very little about horses.

Since starting the retreat center and filling our stable with horses, I learned there is a thick dividing line between mellow horses meant for trail rides with jiggly old guys like me and lightning-fast thoroughbreds meant for galloping fast under the saddles of trained jockeys. The former are mild enough to put a child on; the latter have smoke coming out of their nostrils and are auditioning for the Apocalypse. So when my three friends and I got to the stable, I quickly sized up the situation. We had three mellow horses and one Apocalypse thoroughbred racehorse. The first three horses were already saddled up, so I escorted my friends to their rides. Then I grabbed a saddle to put on my ride, trying my best to look like I knew what I was doing. I tried to properly seat my saddle, but I was mostly throwing straps around and tying granny knots on anything I could find. I think I had one strap over this stud's ear and another tied to his tail. I tried to play it cool and act the part so my friends wouldn't get nervous on my behalf.

When it was time to ride, my friends all mounted their horses looking as calm and pleased as a perfect spring afternoon. I took a deep breath, grabbed the horn on the saddle, and threw a leg over my racehorse. That's when things quickly unspooled for me. The moment I made it onto the saddle, the horse took off running and bucking. I couldn't tell which end was up because my head was shaking so violently. I held on for dear life, not knowing I had a better chance of survival by exiting this ride somehow. The longer I stayed in the saddle, the angrier the horse got and the more he jumped and bucked and snorted. It was not eight seconds of glory. It was more like thirty seconds of Bob's feet flying above his head while his bum slammed into the saddle. The horse eventually won the contest and threw me off. Fortunately I landed on my head, which is pretty thick.

My eyes were level with the ground, and as I regained my ability to focus, I could see three pairs of legs sprinting in my direction. I couldn't let on that I really got my bell rung, so I sprang to my feet, laughing. "I'm fine, I'm fine," I said, dusting myself off. "Happens all the time. I do that every day. It's just a thing I do in the mornings to knock the cobwebs off. How did I look?" Meanwhile I was wiping my eyes and ears to see if blood was leaking out.

Here's the thing: I knew I was lying. I was in immense pain, possibly concussed, and wanted to find the nearest hot tub, doctor, gauze wrap, and bottle of ibuprofen. My friends knew I was lying too. They could see the grimace behind the smile.

After that we had a good day together, but later that night I had to ask myself, *Why wasn't I just honest about what I was feeling?* I could have said to my friends, "Give me a minute to figure out what my name is." But instead of being real, I faked it. Being less than authentic didn't come totally from a place of pride for me in that instance, and I bet it doesn't for you all the time either. My reason for being so cheery was simple: Everyone came to have a good time, and I didn't want to be a buzzkill. So rather than showing my pain, I pretended.

I know that acting tough after getting bucked off a horse isn't the highest-stakes example. But what about some of the other issues we deal with? Do you have a friend hiding an addiction? Does your high schooler get vulnerable about their fears, or do they shrink away, afraid to look "less than" someone else? Life can be a wild ride sometimes, and when we get bucked off the horse, we are all tempted to dust ourselves off to keep anyone from seeing the pain underneath. If we want to go deeper in our relationships, we can't go shallow with our authenticity.

———

Because we're talking about getting real, it seems right that I should bring up *Pinocchio*. If you didn't grow up watching this Disney movie or hearing the story, here's a very brief refresher. Pinocchio is a marionette made by a loving woodworker named Geppetto, a charming and grandfatherly type who whittles away in his tiny shop. Geppetto hopes Pinocchio will become a real boy someday, and the story takes off from there, thanks to a fairy who whooshes life into Pinocchio with her wand.

Instead of Pinocchio becoming a flesh-and-blood person, though, he remains an animated version of a wooden toy. He can talk, think, and move, but he is still made of wood. I can relate. We all want to be more real, don't we? There's no blue fairy who can lead us there—we have Jesus for that—but the wisdom she drops on Pinocchio about the path to becoming real still holds a lot of truth. Listen to what she tells him: that becoming real is to become "brave, truthful, and unselfish." I have a theology that is broader than these attributes, but it is certainly inclusive of them. Give some serious thought to welcoming these virtues into your life as you become more real to the people around you.

Pinocchio could go to the library and read books on human physiology, I suppose. He could interview philosophers about the essence of the human experience. He could sit down for coffee with other humans and hear stories about their lives. None of this would make him more human though. Collecting more information about life and even about God is safe because it can create an illusion of progress, but it doesn't make us any more real. I'm not telling you to discount information completely; just know that it will not get you where you need to go all by itself. In fact, merely collecting information, analyzing it, and endlessly tweaking plans can become a form of distraction, a type of procrastination from your real life.

To become more human, you have to undertake the brave work of becoming real. Why not start by being a little more brave, truthful, and unselfish like Pinocchio was instructed to be and see what happens? My bet is that those traits will create a path to the right kinds of relationships, and those friendships will point you to a more meaningful, joyful, and purposeful life.

It's easy to both underestimate and overestimate this work. Let me explain. Becoming more real doesn't have to be an extensive journey, like a trek across a glacier; it can be as accessible as a walk across the street or down the hall to love your neighbor. Try this: Be completely authentic with one person today. Then double your reach and the depth of your conversations tomorrow. Snorkelers stay in the top few feet of the surface in their conversations. Shipwreck divers go as deep as it takes to find the treasure. I promise that if you'll explore what lies below all the surface talk, you'll find some forever friendships—and when you do, you will discover joy and perhaps even your faith all over again.

Don't be discouraged or distracted if you have a couple of relational setbacks on the path to becoming more real. It doesn't mean you are lousy with people. It means you are learning, just like we all are. Don't rule out that there might also be some people who are lousy with you. Be mindful of who you take your cues from. The funny thing about relationships is that the people who stink at them often think they're the best at them. Identify these people in your life, and decide right now to take the amount of influence they have in your life down a notch or two.

Another key to becoming more authentic is being plainspoken about the facts and details of your life. Here's what I mean. If you want to eliminate the distractions and create some relational capital, don't embellish what you are experiencing by shading it one way or the other. Just tell the truth. The fish doesn't need to get bigger every time you tell the story. Go read that story in the Bible about Ananias and Sapphira and see how it worked out for them.[1] They were good and kind and generous, but they weren't honest about *how* generous they were—and it cost them their lives.

Don't spin the events of your life or assume everything you say or do has to be ready for a press release. Be kind but a little unkempt; speak the truth as you see it; risk saying out loud what you really think without running everything through a public relations filter first. When you let your real self out, you will attract the people who like how you uniquely live and see the world. Those are the ones who long for a real relationship with a person like *you*, not a relationship with a version of you that doesn't really even exist.

If you want to clear the distractions from your life, give away acts of unselfish love. Do things without drawing any attention or taking a bow. Jesus told His friends these were the things that would last. Make loving people its own reward without looking for approval or applause. Make unselfish acts of kindness as natural as taking a deep breath. Make this your defining characteristic. Combine this with unabashed truthfulness and acts of courage and bravery, and you will be as real as anyone can ever get.

If we are going to access the most powerful, impactful life available, we have to get ruthless about the obstacles getting in our way. This is hard and can be confusing work sometimes. To be candid, there have been seasons when I avoided this job altogether because it can be an exhausting effort. I know plenty of people—very well-meaning adults who seem very well put together—who have never asked these questions of themselves. But guess what? Their lives also don't look all that interesting, at least from where I'm sitting. They look like they are merely hustling for a payday or a fast car or a nice home, just trying to make it to the weekend or the next vacation—all to the exclusion of purpose. They appear to be repeating the scripts of their ambitious friends' lives . . . or perhaps the lives their parents lived before them. It's like a multigenerational Groundhog Day of distractions that is leading them away from authentic joy.

Look, we all start with the hands we are dealt. Some distractions are outside of us, and we must respond to the ones blocking our paths. Other distractions are implanted in us, or placed in our hearts by the people we have trusted throughout our lives. Still other distractions are the ones we sabotage ourselves with. I have seen this happen most within our surface-level relationships. Here are my questions: How much energy are you wasting constructing an imaginary world you hope will protect you? Are you trying to control all the outcomes and hedge against the massive amount of uncertainty God has baked into life? Are you trading who you really are for a caricature of who you are?

If you've ever heard of Pavlov's dog, then you will remember Pavlov's work around conditioned responses. Pavlov was a scientist who ran an experiment in which he rang a bell and then gave food to his dog. The dog eventually connected the bell ringing with something good to follow, which was some food. It wasn't long before Pavlov's dog would start salivating every time the bell rang, kind of like me when I smell pizza.

After enough experiences, we link things to expected results. Perhaps we see "the light coming on" or "hear the bell ringing" and are conditioned to anticipate something good coming our way. Similarly, after some bad things happen, we link those experiences to similar negative results. For instance, after being thrown off a horse, we might declare we'll never ride again. Our minds and hearts are wired to reduce pain and discomfort and increase pleasure and comfort. The Bible tells us as much. Face it: The things we have experienced, both good and bad, shape how we anticipate what will happen next.

Some of us defer our celebrations, happiness, and joy because of a few bad turns we experienced in the past. The fix requires that we first understand why we are doing what we are doing. If we are not aware of the reasons for our behaviors and conditioned responses, we won't be able to change them in any meaningful way and make the kind of progress we want. Sure, it feels easier to ignore what is triggering the fear or apprehension or stress we feel and to hope these feelings will just go away or resolve themselves, but here's the thing: They won't. Sometimes our past just doesn't want to stay in the past anymore. Don't be alarmed when this happens; instead, embrace it, understand it, and replace one conditioned response with a newer, better, more rational, more faithful, and more focused one. Replace accusation with empathy, guilt with compassion, and anger with perspective and grace. This is the power God gives each of us if we will have the guts to be new creations. Simply put, the next version of you can decide not to let the past push you around anymore.

Ask yourself: "What simply can't be deferred any longer in my life?" Are you putting off whatever it is because you were burned last time? Are you afraid? Me, too, sometimes. The fix is to get real about it. Call it out. Name it for what it is. Stop beating yourself up about it and instead, kick it in the pants. Next, replace that old perspective with a newer, more fitting response and get busy being a more authentic version of yourself. If you will do this courageous work, what has dogged you in the past will no longer be able to exert control over you.

When I look at the life of Jesus, I see someone who was willing to question whether the way things were happening was the way things had to keep happening. His entire life was commissioned with the task of changing the way we interacted with God. To do this, Jesus had to become incredibly vulnerable and real and present. He laughed, He cried, He broke ranks with the social norms of the time.

He invited the people around Him to do the same, and He is still extending this invitation to us: to drop our preconceived notions and the layers of protection we have ensconced ourselves with, whether they be religion or social status or money. Jesus cut straight to the heart of the matter; He constantly removed the distractions that kept people from seeing Him for who He really was; and when they did see Him, they found love and deeper purpose. He shows us how to transform from a wooden toy to flesh and blood.

He's inviting you to do the same. Buck the trends; defy the world's assumption that you will maintain the status quo. Choose to go deep instead. Quit merely complying with everyone's expectations about who you should be. Make a little noise if you need to. Decide you will transform who you are from a puppet to a real person. Discovering and living your true purpose can only happen when you're brave enough to cut the strings and be real with a handful of other people around you.

Pavlov's dog taught us a lot to be sure, but just because the "light comes on" or we "hear a bell ringing" with a familiar encounter or circumstance, we can't let our past have the last word anymore. Our past can certainly point in the direction of our future, but we have enough agency to declare that the past doesn't control us. The game isn't fixed, nor is the outcome predetermined. Live in a state of constant anticipation of finding a new gear and a better response than you've had in the past. Certainly, you should remember the past and learn from it, but leave a little room for God to show up with some new adventures, some grace, and some new outcomes. Live an intentionally surprised life.

During the siege of Leningrad, sadly, Pavlov's dogs were eaten.[2] I bet they didn't see that coming. As you journey forward, a couple of good things will come your way, and a few bad ones too. Don't be too quick to respond with a bunch of assumptions about what will happen next. This will only distract you from what God has up His sleeve. Have your head on a swivel to see other outcomes that might be possible, even if improbable. Learn from the past and then get back to living in constant anticipation of what God could have for you next.

CHAPTER 14

THE MISADVENTURES
OF A SERIAL REJECT

See unexpected circumstances as surprises,
and what seems like disappointment
will become an invitation.

There's this organization I love that reaches out to young people in high school. Their mission is to engage kids with the love of God without expecting them to have it all together before they are accepted. The reason I love this organization is because I was one of those kids once. One of the leaders had a major impact in my life. He knew me from high school and could probably sense I was feeling like an outsider. I was contemplating dropping out of school and getting a job. One day this leader was there for me when I showed up on his doorstep and, without any planning or preparation, joined me on a road trip even though he was a newlywed. I mean, who do you know who does that? I should probably apologize to his bride for being a confused teenager, but she already knew that about me.

This leader's impact on my life changed everything. I stayed in high school and went to college too. I became a leader with the same organization in college and engaged kids to hopefully steer them on a collision course with God's love, just like someone had done for me. After college I wanted to get a job working on staff at their main offices. I wanted to be more than just a volunteer with this organization, so I raised my own salary by asking friends and family for donations. I wouldn't cost them anything, so it seemed like a pretty good deal for everyone involved. I was full of energy, committed to the mission of the organization, and really good at breaking down barriers with kids.

I applied for the job and got turned down flat. *Wait, what?* I wasn't mad, just befuddled and a little hurt. It never feels good to put yourself out there and have someone say, "Uh, no thanks." Especially when you're free labor, there's literally no risk for them, and no one else was applying for the job. I never got a satisfying explanation. On reflection, I now understand that I'm not great at taking directions, and it was probably good judgment on their part to turn me away. I wouldn't have done whatever they told me to do, and we all would have been unhappy. I just couldn't see it at the time; it felt like rejection.

If you were in my position, how would you respond to such a setback? Would you sulk and complain? Would you let off some steam? Would you blame it on God or see it as forces of darkness arrayed against you? Or, would you see the rejection as an opportunity to learn something more about yourself, take a new path in your life, and perhaps develop a couple of new skills? I'll be the first to admit that inexplicable disappointments can gut our confidence.

But here's the thing. I didn't let this rejection become an identifying factor in my life, and I don't want these types of setbacks to define who you are either.

Some people let disappointments turn into distractions. Don't be the kind of person who falls for that trap. Stop thinking about how unfair life can be, and turn the letdowns into lessons and the disappointments into determination. So you didn't land the job you wanted or the relationship you desired or the opportunity you felt you had earned. When we encounter setbacks, we get to decide to be the kind of people who get busy—not bitter—and start moving in another direction. Stop dwelling on the curveball you missed and get your head back in the game. Another pitch will come your way soon. Be ready to swing at it.

Since I didn't get the job at the organization, I decided to apply to law school instead. I was ambitious and optimistic and wasn't going to let my disappointment wrap me around the axle. I asked at least a dozen law schools if they would let me in, and you want to know how many said yes? Think of a round number. None. Zero. Nada. Zilch.

Eventually, after a sit-in, I talked one of the law schools into taking a risk on me. Three years later I graduated and passed the bar exam in several states. I put my head down, worked hard, and became a partner in a medium-sized law firm in San Diego. I eventually quit that job to start my own law firm. By the way, I didn't ask for permission to leave the security of my job, and you don't need permission to quit yours either. I picked my life and backfilled my career rather than doing the opposite, which I had seen so many others do.

The law firm I started did really well over the next several years. We grew as other lawyers and staff joined us. We opened offices in several states, and everything was looking up. We specialized in representing nonprofits, and one day the idea came to me: *What if we offered our services for free to that organization that reached me in high school?* They had a lot of physical properties and donors and staff, so I suspected their legal wrangling and paperwork would be mountainous. The thought of helping out felt really good to me because the organization still held a special place in my heart. I accepted that I wasn't the right fit to join them years before, but maybe now that I was an accomplished attorney, I could save them a ton of money. Besides, I would do it for *free*, so what would they have to lose? I called them up to share this generous offer with them, certain it was a slam-dunk proposal. Get this: They turned me down again. *Wait, what?*

I didn't get an explanation (again), but I suspect they were all set with the really smart lawyers they already had. My guess is that the free work I offered was a better deal, but my generous offer didn't need to be accepted to still be important—and yours doesn't either. Building a case against other people when they decline your offers and availability will only distract you. Go with obedience instead. It will outperform recognition every time.

All of this is just a different version of what has probably already happened to you a dozen times. I'm not blowing sunshine at you here, but how would your life be different if you looked at disappointing outcomes as enticing opportunities? Because the truth is, God knows *exactly* what He's doing, and He is never surprised. Disappointments are often divine redirections, but sometimes to get where you want to go when the road washes out, you have to get busy and build a new path.

Disappointments don't make you a victim; they prove that you are a participant, and participation is what we are called to—not success or job titles or acknowledgment. Even in the face of outcomes you don't want, you have unstoppable, irrevocable agency to take the next few courageous steps. Don't just agree with me about these things; live into these truths with gusto. You can pivot anytime you want, knowing ultimately that the affirmation and validation you may crave can only come from God. And here is a magnificent, irrefutable headline: He already approves of you.

I couldn't be their staff member or their lawyer, so I decided I would just be this organization's friend and good neighbor. If you've read any of my other books, you know about our family lodge in Canada that we built next door to a camp owned by this same outfit. You know why it's there? Because years ago I met a special woman who was a leader, and she captivated my heart and changed the course of my life. (You know her as Sweet Maria.) The camp and our lodge are surrounded by thousands of square miles of beautiful virgin-growth cedar trees. Logging companies love these trees because they can charge a lot of money for them. Over the years, the loggers would try to buy the land around the camp and our home so they could harvest the timber. But I couldn't bear the thought of a clear-cut mountainside in a place that was supposed to be pristine and inspiring for generations of explorers.

Anytime my law firm won a big case I would take a portion of the proceeds and buy blocks of forest surrounding the camp, one hundred acres at a time. I did this for twenty years and ended up protecting a great deal of the forest in the inlet, and then we gave much of the property to the organization who had turned me down so many times. Now it's impossible for anyone to ever ruin this special place.

I doubt I could have done these things if this organization had hired me all those years ago for free as a leader or for free as a lawyer. It turns out I make a much better neighbor than employee. I'm betting God knew this would be true as I reflect on how one obstacle after another was inexplicably thrown in my way on the path I thought I wanted. These disappointments I thought were roadblocks to my ambitions were actually plowing the road toward what I wanted even more—results that would prove to be much more lasting. If something doesn't go your way, don't get sour. Get creative. Counteract your disappointment with imagination and joy and vision and hard work. You'll find a way to make good on your beautiful intentions later.

I guess what I'm saying is this: Don't be distracted by delays. Instead, start counting on them, banking on them, embracing and enjoying them. Don't curse the wind; let it fill your sails. If you have lost your job, I know it can be a stressful time. What if you could turn the time between jobs into the vacation time you could never get off before? Perhaps you can recast some portion of your un-employment as fun-employment. I get it; you're thinking all of this is easier to say than it is to do, and you know what? You're right. Still, the people who understand the power of purpose and joy do it anyway. They have released the notion that everything is going to work out the way they planned it and are enjoying the delightful and uncertain ride.

———

As a young guy, one area in my life where I had to practice extreme faith was romantic relationships. I was what some call a "late bloomer" when it came to dating. I'm not sure this is an accurate way to describe me. There's this flower called the "corpse flower." It's the largest flower in the world and has that name because it smells really, really bad and only blooms once every forty years. That's how my dating life felt; I stunk at it. Maybe I should have taken more showers too. Who knows? I certainly had a lot more bulb than bloomer in me.

My ambition in junior high school was to go out on a date. It never happened, but I had high hopes for high school. My ambition never really materialized in any significant way in high school, either, but there was always college, right? I managed to squeeze four years of college into five but still had no luck dating. I met Sweet Maria in my second year of law school and was immediately smitten. She was a part of the same organization I had unsuccessfully tried to join so many times, so I knew we had plenty in common. I knew deep down in my bone marrow that she was the one I had been waiting for since before I had pimples. So after we had been around each other a few times, I asked her out on a date.

To this day I'm convinced every girl took the same class on saying no, because that's exactly what Sweet Maria said. She wasn't mean about it, and we stayed friends. But here's the thing. I knew what I wanted, and I was tenacious, so I kept looking for more chances to be anywhere in her orbit. Pursuing Sweet Maria felt purposeful, and while I was pursuing her, I remained completely undistracted by the strong historical possibility, if not certainty, it wouldn't work out.

I heard Sweet Maria was going to be at a camp in the mountains nearby leading ten high school girls who would be volunteering at a weekend women's retreat. I'm no dummy and saw an opportunity. I immediately rounded up ten high school guys to volunteer at the camp so I would have a reason to be near Sweet Maria without looking like a stalker. On the first night of the retreat, an elderly woman's pacemaker stopped, and she face-planted in her spaghetti. She was gone, and not just a little gone. She was full-on, go toward the light, ascend to heaven, meet Saint Peter, capital-G gone. But get this: I knew how to do CPR, so for the next thirty minutes, I pumped on her chest and blew into her wrinkled lips until the ambulance arrived. And it worked. The lady who keeled over opened her eyes as we touched lips again, and we both figured out she wasn't dead. It was hardly the first kiss I was hoping for that weekend, and while it wasn't quite a Lazarus-level occurrence, it was close enough to get Sweet Maria's attention. She must have been thinking to herself, *This guy isn't much to look at, but he can be useful in a pinch.*

Spoiler alert: I persisted and eventually got that first kiss from Sweet Maria. Thirty-four years of marriage and three kids later, we found out that this same camp where things got started was up for sale. I hadn't been back to the camp in almost forty years, and it hadn't been updated or renovated in a while. It was looking more than a little frayed around the edges. In some places it smelled like three hundred fourteen-year-old boys had been living there for decades without taking any showers. With some good friends we bought the camp, got the squirrels out of the walls, stripped the rooms down to the studs, and moved a few walls around to turn the rooms into suites. We replaced the plywood bunk beds with queen-sized beds, brought in leather furniture, and hung oil paintings on as many empty walls as we could find. We turned the place into a really beautiful high-end retreat center, and we were excited to throw the doors open and welcome people to the rest and clarity they needed. We knew it would be a place where people could get away from the distractions in their lives and find their joy again.

We picked a grand opening date, and I started blowing up the balloons, which is my go-to when I'm excited and don't know what to do. "This is going to be terrific," I kept saying over and over again to anyone who would listen. We were filled with an almost unbearable amount of anticipation. The COVID-19 pandemic and the subsequent shutdowns happened one month before The Oaks Retreat Center was scheduled to open. We went from big visions and grand plans to sixty thousand square feet of empty buildings on a couple of hundred acres in Southern California, which isn't cheap. We had more tumbleweeds blowing through the retreat center than people, and we were losing a truly stunning amount of money each month. It was almost two years before we could host any guests at our retreat center.

This didn't happen to you, of course, but a version of this happens to all of us at different times and in different ways. At some point, we have a terrific idea; we can't wait to release it into the world; and it seems like everything is going just great—right up until it doesn't. Know what I mean? This is how so much of life works, and we're going to need to figure out a strategy in advance to deal with letdowns. If we don't, we'll be so distracted by the momentary catastrophes that we'll miss the possibilities that reside right next door. When the inevitable happens, resist giving God a list of your grievances. Instead, take inventory of what you've already got and what is already adjacent to you.

Next to The Oaks there was a beautiful valley with a huge field. At one point it was part of a famous horse racing and training center that had produced two Kentucky Derby winners. The field had an old abandoned barn, an overgrown horse racetrack, and one hundred acres of pastures. Rather than focusing on the retreat center that wasn't working, we got busy with a new plan. We got the horse property, made it part of our retreat center, and hired a horse trainer named Efrim. He's like a centaur. Half man, half horse. At least it seems that way because of how much he knows about horses and how good he is with our guests. People now send us their horses from all around the world so he can train them. When we hit a roadblock at the camp, instead of bailing on the dream, we looked to what was already adjacent to us.

Before starting the equestrian center, my only interaction with a horse had been in front of the grocery store when I was five. It was made of fiberglass, and it rocked back and forth for a couple of minutes when I put a nickel in it. I had never been on a real horse or even fed a horse. When the horses started to arrive, I didn't know which end to put the hay in. But guess what? I figured it out and you will figure out what you need to know to move forward.

We were still losing our shirts owning an empty retreat center, but we were making bank training horses. Even when all the circumstances pointed in another direction, we resisted the urge to freak out or get distracted by what wasn't working. We didn't wait for permission to pivot from our beautiful failing vision to one that was viable; we got busy finding a possibility next door. You can bet your life on this: Your daring ideas and the disappointments you experience will be catnip for new opportunities and additional paths forward toward your lasting ambitions—if only you will have the courage not to relent.

Once we had our horse operation up and running, a woman called and said she had a racehorse to give me. *Terrific. I have a barn to put it in, so that's perfect.* I didn't have any intelligent questions to ask her about the horse, so to fill the dead airtime I asked her what color it was. She dropped the horse off the next day, and it turned out to be brown with a black tail. I just told you everything I knew about the horse.

Later that year someone said it was time to think about breeding some of the horses that had arrived. We researched the lineage of the brown-and-black horse I was given, and get this: Turns out she is the great-great-granddaughter of Secretariat, the winner of the Triple Crown and one of the most famous horses in racing history. I kid you not. We called the woman and asked if she knew the racehorse she gave me was royalty. She paused and said, "Yes, I just wanted to surprise you." *Well, check that box,* I thought.

What if heaven is itching to surprise you right now? What if God's plan for you is the absence of any clear plan at all? If you knew everything you needed to do, you wouldn't need faith anymore. Practice not freaking out as you watch the unexpected circumstances God brings unfolding in front of you.

We will all try things. Some of these things will work and more than a few won't. Look at what I've shared with you in just this chapter. These adventures and misadventures haven't just involved camps and dates and horses; they have spanned jobs, careers, relationships, and business ventures. Let me state the obvious. Some of the jobs you want you'll get, and with others you'll be turned down flat. The same goes for relationships. If you're as bad at dating as I was, perhaps doubly so. Don't be fooled into thinking everything that happens to you is a cosmic battle between good and evil. The author G. K. Chesterton famously said, "Idolatry is committed, not merely by setting up false gods, but also by setting up false devils."[1]

God is in control of everything, but we need to stop being distracted by thinking we can control all the outcomes in our lives. Instead of becoming distracted by surprises, we need to take responsibility where we need to and action where we can. The mistakes we make aren't outtakes to edit *from* our lives; they are bookmarks for the places where we learn the most *about* our lives. I heard this saying the other day: "Experience is the thing we gain the moment after we needed it."[2] I can relate. We can't control all the ways things turn out, but we can influence them if we will keep showing up undistracted and in anticipation that God is not only in front of us and behind us but also beside us and with us. This is going to take all the focus, patience, resolve, and perspective you can muster. Don't let surprising and unexpected outcomes rob you of the chance to gain experience and wisdom. Trust me, you'll probably need it for your next attempt.

If you're like me, the way things unfold in your life can seem at times like one continuous strand of inexplicable nos. But you can choose to see these circumstances as yeses to what's adjacent to you for two reasons: God's got you, and you've got this.

CHAPTER 15

STOP CHASING THE HORSE

Everything you need is much closer to home than you think.

One of our friends heard about the setback we were having with the camp being closed and sent us a movie called *We Bought a Zoo*. If you haven't seen it, do yourself a favor and watch it soon because you are going to love it. There is a scene in which the recently widowed father is explaining to his confused and distressed son how life works. He tells him with the voice of a concerned and caring father: "All you need is twenty seconds of insane courage. Just twenty seconds of embarrassing bravery and it will change everything."[1] I agree. And my questions for you are: What would it look like if you had twenty seconds of insane courage? What would twenty seconds of embarrassing bravery create in your life?

Not far away from The Oaks there was a wealthy guy who had a huge ranch where he raised racehorses. He decided to sell his facility and found other wealthy people to buy his expensive horses. One day I was over at his ranch to buy a used manure spreader. I delighted in knowing that by afternoon I would finally be the guy on the green John Deere tractor pulling a big piece of equipment down the highway and slowing down traffic. I grinned as I thought about the magnificent journey I had taken from a trial lawyer to my much more delightful and fitting role as a ranch hand. With my manure spreader in tow, I knew there must be a lawyer joke in there somewhere.

There was only one racehorse left to be sold. The remaining horse caught my attention because it was *huge*. I mean, *block the sun* huge. He made other horses look like miniature poodles. I was certain I could put a sign on the road for people to come see it, like for the World's Largest Ball of Twine in Kansas or the Corn Palace in South Dakota.

Horses are measured in hands, which is exactly what it sounds like. This is an old practice from when there were no standard measuring tools. Today, a hand is standardized as four inches, which is measured between the ground and the bottom of the neck. This horse was seventeen hands, which is like an eleven-foot, six-inch center in basketball. At full height from hoof to head, this horse was more than eight feet tall. Any way I sized this horse up, it was an imposing animal.

The owner asked if I wanted to buy his expensive racehorse, and I laughed as I pulled out my wallet. I had a single dollar bill in it and pulled it out, letting him know this was all I had on me. "Sold!" he said without hesitation, reaching out his right hand to me to seal the deal.

"Really?" I yelped in shock.

"Yep, he's all yours."

Evidently, the reason he was parting so cheaply with the horse was because it had injured a tendon in one of its legs, and the owner figured its racing days were over.

After the deal was struck and we arranged how to transfer the horse, I realized I had overlooked one small detail. Horse trailers are made for normal horses. But this was like a giraffe-horse, and we didn't have a large enough trailer. After some cajoling, cramming, and squeezing, we eventually smooshed him into the one we had and took him back to The Oaks training center. I named our new horse Red because that's his color, and because calling him "great big one-dollar horse" sounded a little too generic and felt like leaving the price tag on your new car.

Before throwing a saddle on Red, I took him out for a walk holding on to his lead rope. As we walked into one of the nearby pastures, Red got spooked and reared up on his back legs. He was huge before, but now he was straight-up ginormous and extremely scary. I was standing underneath him, wondering if I would be adding "getting trampled" to my various life experiences. For a second, with his hooves waving, it looked like he was about to deal cards. Then his front legs came down—thankfully not on me—and he ripped the lead rope out of my hands and bolted across the one-hundred-acre field. Not sure what to do, I started running after him.

It wasn't long before I was completely winded and realized the absolute folly of this pursuit. I mean, I probably couldn't catch a carnival pony let alone a full-on racehorse. I stopped, bent over double sucking gulps of air, and thought to myself, *What am I doing?* Instead of continuing to chase the horse across the field, I went back to the barn and got a few carrots—not for him, but for me. Fifteen minutes later Red trotted back to the barn.

The reason I'm telling you this story is because that little episode taught me an important lesson about distractions. I realized that sometimes you need to stop chasing the horse and go back to the barn.

What have you been chasing? Are you pursuing acceptance?

Popularity? A relationship? How about a dream job or career? Have you been running across the fields of your life looking for permission or validation or approval? What if you were to stop running after things you are never going to catch and just return to the basics of your life: your faith, family, purpose, joy, and your most authentic life? In other words, go back to the barn and give up chasing the things you aren't going to catch or that aren't worth corralling anyway.

Going back to the barn doesn't mean you lack ambition, nor does it mean you are bailing on things that are important to you. It just means you're becoming more assured about who God made you to be. Imagine what would be possible if you tapped the brakes in your exhausting life, regrouped, caught your breath, and returned to the basics—because this is where all the good stuff usually already resides in your life.

There is a letter in the Bible that Paul wrote to Jewish Christians. He reminded them that they were surrounded by what he called "a great cloud of witnesses."[2] I like the visual. Paul told them to set aside anything slowing them down, tripping them up, or wearing them out and instead focus on the things God had for them. If you find that passage, you'll notice that Paul didn't encourage people to look at what God was doing in someone else's life and compare it to theirs. It's like Paul was telling them (and us) to stop chasing the horse and head back to the barn. What if the barn for you is where you can lose the distractions, be surrounded by safe people, and find renewed clarity about what really matters?

I was positive that my new horse would find its way back to the barn, but I don't know if you will because the decision is completely yours to make. So what do you say? Let's get you back to a safe place that you can call home. You may find that things you have been desperate to catch might actually meet you there if you will stop running so hard.

When I was in college, I spent a couple of months hitchhiking as a way to see the country. It was a different time then, and a lot of people in my generation traveled that way. It's hard to imagine people being so trusting now. I made it to New England and was often riding between total strangers. Some of them were nice and generous; others were just plain odd. But I was happy as long as I got to my destination without having too many creepy things happen. Besides, I was looking a little creepy myself as a nineteen-year-old with flaming red hair down to his shoulders, torn jeans, and a stained T-shirt. I didn't need much—just a ride and a breath mint—and I honestly could have used a pair of boots that would get me through the winter because my beat-up tennis shoes were falling apart.

When someone pulled over to give me a lift, I would try to size them up before I got in the car; no doubt they were trying to do the same with me. Outside Bangor, Maine, I held my thumb out for a long time before a truck pulled over with an older, smaller man at the wheel. He had gentle eyes, and even his bushy eyebrows and beard seemed kind to me. I'm not sure why, but they did. I climbed in the passenger seat. "My name is Don," the driver said, sticking out his hand a little tentatively. Don apparently didn't have a last name, and I was okay with that. Kind of like Jesus or MacGyver or Cher, I figured.

We made chitchat down the highway. He asked me about my adventures and I asked him about his life. What I learned surprised me. Don told me he was a hermit who lived alone in the woods. *Then what are you doing out here picking me up?* I instantly thought. I won't lie; I thought maybe this might go badly. If they'd had podcasts back then, I might have imagined becoming the subject of an eight-part show about a young, happy hitchhiker abducted by a hermit. Actually, that sounds like a pretty good premise now. Maybe I'll take it to Netflix.

I had heard about hermits but had never met one. I became quite curious about Don. What was his house like? Did he have a house? Did he have a pet? Was it a hermit crab? I'm just saying, it would've made sense. Did he talk to squirrels? Could he play thumb wars with himself? My mind was racing.

I didn't realize how long I had been waiting for a ride because as soon as I got into Don's car, it started turning to dusk. It would be nighttime soon, and I hadn't reached any kind of destination where I could stay overnight. Don must have been doing the same calculations. "It's gonna be dark soon. Do you have a place to stay tonight?" he asked. I answered no, and he nonchalantly invited me to stay at his house. There I was riding shotgun with a guy who looked like a mix of Yosemite Sam and Father Christmas. In a moment of brilliant foolishness, I accepted his invitation.

We drove awhile longer, and it turned completely to nighttime. His driveway was an unmarked gravel road entrance off a two-lane state highway. If I got into serious trouble, I would have no way of communicating where I was. Not that it mattered, because as we made our way down the narrow "driveway" to his house, Don told me that he had no phone. Or electricity. Or plumbing. He got his power from a propane tank that was enough to heat a small oven. He drew his water by the bucket from a well behind the house, and he bartered with his neighbors for everything he needed. Talk about a life without distractions.

We finally arrived, and the look of the house was probably what you'd expect. It was a small shack with a sloped roof overhanging a front porch. There was a single window next to the front door with a faint battery-operated light shining out into the surrounding woods. I was a little nervous to know how many beds were inside. I doubted it could handle anything more than a couple of cots. Don pulled up to the quaint structure, we both got out, and he shut the door behind us once we were inside.

Obviously, since I'm writing about this, I didn't die. In fact, I had a great time with Don. I wasn't sure how things would go, but I was pleasantly surprised. I didn't spend just one night with Don. I spent a month there.

You might be wondering why I stayed so long. I'm not sure I have a clear-cut answer for you. I was young and looking for adventures. I also didn't have anywhere else to be. I was dirt-poor, and as it turned out Don was kind and wise and caring. I never learned why he became a hermit or if he had anyone else in his life. But the fact that he invited me into his home suggested that maybe he needed a friend—as we all do in some measure. I was a curious guy, and as long as my life wasn't too endangered and I was having an adventure, I was game for pretty much anything, anytime, anywhere, including an extended stay at what I started thinking of as the Hotel Hermit— "Where the cots are free and you don't have to flush a toilet."

Don and I quickly settled into a daily rhythm with various chores divided between us. The day would start with making candlestick holders that we would drop off at different people's houses later in the day. We made candlestick bases by cutting round pieces of copper, then pounding them with a hammer into a tree stump with an indentation. We then heated brass rods with a torch and bent them before brazing a round plate to catch the dripping wax. Finally, we cut a piece of copper pipe to make a ring to hold the wax candle and brazed it in place. We would tidy the house, make a simple breakfast, deliver the candlestick holders, and then much later in the day read for a while. It was magical in its simplicity, and we were practically a couple.

When the candleholders were delivered, each family would invite us to take what we needed from their vegetable gardens or woodpiles. One house was locally famous for its large rhubarb garden. We would pick the stalks, take them home, and make rhubarb pies to drop off the next morning in exchange for still more veggies, bars of soap, lead pencils, and butter. We had just about anything we needed (except toilet paper). One time Don parlayed several pies into a used truck tire, and another time, a car battery. The pies we made were like sugar-saturated bitcoin for us. I figured this was how Don had worked out his hermit life—using what he had or knew how to create to get almost anything he needed.

———

I think most of us want our faith to be simply more real, more dynamic, and more connected to the people around us. The problem is, we don't use what we already have to get what we really need. We complicate our lives and distract ourselves with things we don't need or want. We live in a community of people yet we live like hermits. We have families who love us but we live like we're alone. We think we can trade good conduct for God's grace, but we can't and when we try to, it makes us look like orphans. We all want our faith to look like it's working, but we overlook the beauty and authenticity of letting the people around us know when we are lost and hurting.

I suppose the same thing happens in our faith communities every day. We want to know who we can trust and who we ought to pass by, who we ought to go with and who we should avoid. In short, we're all trying to figure out how to live out our faith and who to do it with. God has not left us alone; He's given us each other. He's given us communities of faith to go deeper with, and He's given us His Son. In other words, we don't need to live like hermits anymore.

We need to return to the most real versions of our faith and the most authentic versions of ourselves.

There are a lot of Christians who live like hermits in their personal expressions of faith. Perhaps at some point they became distracted and started caring more about what their faith looked like than what it actually was. Maybe their opinions about people they disagreed with started blocking their view of these same people God made in His image. Possibly they got burned along the way by someone who claimed to be following Jesus but acted otherwise—someone who said they loved God but acted as if they didn't like the people He made.

It was fall in Maine and the leaves were just beginning to turn colors. It was time for me to leave, and soon Don would give me a ride to the highway so I could start hitchhiking south. We both woke up early, had huge slices of rhubarb pie, slipped into his truck, and headed back down the gravel driveway. We said our goodbyes, and as I got out of the car, Don reached behind the back seat and then handed me a bag. Inside were a pair of his boots to get me through the winter. I've still got them. It was a tender reminder that if we're willing to show up, God will provide us what we need and someone to share it with.

We are all chasing something, and some of us are spending a weird amount of time running from things. As I reflect on that time of my life, I wonder what I was chasing and if those things were worth catching or better to let go of. I bet you know the feeling, and it's okay if you don't have it all figured out. In fact, if you think you do, that's when I would start to worry. Even in college I knew deep down that I didn't want a typical life. I wanted to live off-script. With Don I ended up living off-grid, too, for just a little while. The day I met him, all I thought I needed was a ride and pair of boots. God delivered to me a lot more than these things, and He showed me how I could go much deeper in my faith too. Both Don and I needed to risk a little to make those lessons happen. If you want to go deeper in your faith, perhaps you'll need a little risk too. My time with Don showed me that stepping out of life's typical distractions could clarify where I wanted to go. Try it sometime. Maybe you don't need to stick out your thumb and start hitchhiking, but perhaps you could stick out your hand and greet a total stranger, love them without an agenda, and walk away changed.

To live a life of immense purpose you have to stop chasing what's simply available. Instead, head back to whatever sanctuary you have—a family, a home, a friendship, a treehouse, whatever—and set aside everything else vying for your attention. Only with that focus and the delight of who God made you to be can you find your way to the life you have been imagining.

CHAPTER 16

DRIVEN OUT OF THE SHALLOWS

An unexamined life is a fog of distraction that obscures our whole identity; only the brutally honest are willing to see a newer, better, bigger picture.

My great-grandfather was on his way home from work when he was hit by a train. What are the chances? It's odd having this kind of luck in your family tree. You wonder if it skips a generation and you could be next. According to the family lore, the people who found him put him in a wheelbarrow, carried him back to his house, and tipped him over on the porch where my distant relatives found him the next morning. Apparently they didn't even knock, but I can't blame them.

Almost a century later, I was a lawyer and was working on a case that had me in eastern Oregon where my great-grandfather had lived. I had spent months searching for a guy who swindled quite a few people out of a lot of money in a real estate deal. Years earlier he had skipped town after his business went south, assumed a new identity, and left hundreds of people holding the bag for the millions he made off with. He was so crooked I was sure they would need to screw him into the ground someday when he died. He did a pretty good job disappearing too. It had been years, and I wondered if I would ever catch up to him.

I caught a break when his wife subscribed to the magazine *Redbook* under their previous name by mistake. My private investigators had put out alerts, triggers, and trip wires all over the web for their names. The magazine subscription gave me a return address, so I knew exactly where to serve the legal summons. I had him served with a subpoena to show up for a deposition in the small Oregon town where he was hiding. I bet when he learned how I found him it made for a stressful dinner discussion with his wife. In case you've never heard of it, a deposition is legally binding testimony that a lawyer can submit to court as fact without getting a person on the witness stand. If you can take someone's deposition, it's the same thing as getting called as a witness in court.

When we arrived for the deposition, the first few questions I asked him were about his family tree. This way I would know how to find him if he went missing again. He told me about his brothers and sisters and the names of his parents. Then he told me the names of his grandparents and others a little higher in the branches, and things started to get a little weird. The higher we got in his family tree, the more the names started sounding strangely familiar to me. I asked a few more pointed questions with a growing sense that I was uncovering something important. It turns out he was related to me. Yikes! Again, what are the chances?

When the deposition was over and everyone was packing up,

I asked if he had ever heard about the tragic thing that happened to my great-grandfather, the one who got hit by the train. I asked if he had a resting place (other than the porch) that I could visit to pay my respects. The man laughed and said, "He didn't get hit by a train. He ran out on the family, deserting them in the high desert of eastern Oregon." Then it clicked. The family, abandoned and ashamed, came up with a clever and gruesome story to explain their awful circumstance. They had made up a cover story for the pain they experienced. Evidently, everyone on this particular branch of my whacked family knew it was untrue—except for me. Some lies die hard.

In the end, my crooked relative paid back every penny he took. He didn't do this because he was a good guy but because I was a pretty good lawyer. At least this is the story I've told myself.

We don't have many family reunions. Or if they are happening, I haven't been invited. That's okay, I guess. Maybe I'll be taking more depositions someday, and we can catch up then.

It's unsettling how we tell ourselves stories to paper over the cracks. Or sometimes we don't acknowledge any story whatsoever and we drown our shameful moments in total silence, hoping they'll just go away. Here's another quick example from when I was young.

My dad only has nine and a half fingers. He is a great father, a kind and humble guy, a good friend of mine, and my next-door neighbor. Evidently, when he was a brave young man in army boot camp, they were being trained on how to throw grenades. They had these practice versions that exploded but not with as much wallop as a real grenade would. I bet the instructions were pretty straight-forward: step one, pull the pin; step two, throw. My dad got the first thing right, but not the second. The grenade went off in his hand, and he lost half a finger as a result.

When I was growing up, we never talked about it. Not even

once. I learned years later it was a practice grenade. My dad was and is a courageous guy, so he probably didn't want to make a big deal out of his injury. He knew what happened, but I didn't, so I made up my own story to explain it to myself. Get this: I convinced myself I had too many fingers. Crazy, right? But that's what we do when we don't know the truth and shroud the not-knowing in silence. We make up stories to normalize the unknown; we construct alternate realities that are easier for our hearts and minds to understand. Thinking I had too many fingers at such a young age was a reasonable explanation in the absence of an explanation from my dad. I get what happened. My dad loved me and was trying to be a great father by not talking about his injury. I know it seems ridiculous, but the story I made up seemed true and made sense to my young brain. Do you remember Thanksgiving time in elementary school? The art project was *always* making a turkey with your outstretched fingers. My feathers weren't as long as everyone else's. For my turkey, I would fold my ring finger over in half because my dad didn't have half of his.

When we make up stories to explain what we don't understand, we create further confusion for ourselves and the people around us. It gives us a false sense of control, but in truth, we have deceived ourselves with a subtle lie. We concoct a believable story that is easier than the painful or more complicated truth.

An adult brain weighs just about three pounds. If you've got a really big one, it will tip the scales at about four and a half pounds. My question is this: What are you filling your brain with? Are you carrying around several pounds of distractions and made-up stories in your head? Annie Dillard, in her book *The Writing Life*, said something like: "Be careful what you learn for that is what you will know."[1] If you only learn half-truths you can only live half a life. To live fully you need the whole truth about who you are because only truth will make you clear-eyed about where you're going.

The trouble is that we don't always get to choose what we believe about ourselves. Much of it is imprinted on us by our parents, pastors, teachers, and friends before we have the wherewithal to say, "Hey, wait a minute, that doesn't sound right." Later, we spend a lot of time and exert a lot of emotional energy trying to untangle the stories we've been told or to fill in the gaps for the stories no one will tell us.

Try this exercise. Think about yourself when you were five, ten, fifteen, and twenty. If you're much older, think about thirty and forty. (If you're as old as I am, going much further will hurt your brain.) What would you say to yourself at those stages to give yourself access to the truth you might need later?

"Elmo is a hand puppet" (to the five-year-old).

"You'll make the team next year. Just keep believing" (to the ten-year-old).

"I know it hurts now, but the right one will come along later" (to the fifteen-year-old).

"It's okay to be scared. You'll do better than barely pay the rent. Trust me" (to the twenty-year-old).

"If you keep working this hard, you'll miss out on what matters most to you" (to the thirty-year-old).

"Your life doesn't fall apart when you make that big move to that lower-paying job in the career you always wanted" (to the forty-year-old).

These are all hypothetical examples obviously (except for the one about Elmo, who's real). But my guess is if we could go back, what we would do is dispel myths and misguided beliefs that were somehow grafted into our identities. We would save ourselves the trouble and heartache of living and carrying them with us. Be honest; we would also probably tell ourselves how to wager on every Super Bowl and when to buy Apple and Amazon stock. I'm just saying. We would want our lives to be truer and more streamlined with the realities we eventually learned the hard way.

Now, try one more exercise with me. What do you need to hear right now if your future self could come back to help you? I mean the you of today, the you of *right now.*

I bet you know some truths that you need to accept but feel too afraid to grasp. They're lurking under the surface of your heart and mind. They keep pawing at the door asking for entry, but you hesitate to let them in because of what you believe they will cost you. Let me ask you this: What's better—trudging forward in a half-truth or thriving in a messy full-truth? I know what I'm picking and think you do too.

Some people see themselves guided by destiny or fate or good luck or some combination of these. Others are betting on enough unexpended karma to pull them through. I wouldn't bet the house on these. I have put all my belief in trusting that Jesus is still alive and active in the world. There are some high-level cognitive explanations for how the world works, but in the end, it is people and experiences that shape us. Maybe it's better to say *what we absorb* from these people and experiences is what shapes us. Understanding how we're wired will help us avoid distraction and find joy and purpose in our lives.

We make up rules to hold the stories in place like scaffolding, but the scaffolding we constructed can become a jail. These rules we made up are there to support the stories we made up; and the stories we made up to explain the events we couldn't understand when we were younger become the distractions that separate us from ourselves and everyone else. We all need to ask ourselves at some point whether the stories and rules we constructed are serving us any longer. If we are brave enough to say their shelf life has expired, we can thank them for the temporary help they provided (however fraught it might have been) and then toss them in the waste bin.

Like yours, my parents were amateurs. If you have kids, you are too. If you don't have kids yet, you may get your chance to be a rookie at raising kids someday. My parents wanted me to behave, which I totally understand. I was an energetic kid who always seemed to have burned off his eyebrows with some kind of explosion the day before. I wasn't a handful; I was two arms full and a lot of work to raise. When I did things my parents approved of, they gave me love and affirmation because they were terrific parents. It felt great, as it was intended to. When I behaved in a way they didn't approve of, I made up a story in my mind that they would need to withdraw love from me. They didn't mean for me to feel this, of course, because they were great parents, but I learned a couple of things from the way I perceived the world as a young man.

First, I crafted a story for myself that defined love as something that would be given and withdrawn to control my behavior. I convinced myself that love couldn't be completely trusted; it wasn't an extension of safety and acceptance but a tool to control conduct. Second, and even more insidiously, I became convinced that being left emotionally alone was a possibility in a relationship. It wasn't true for me because my parents loved me, but it felt true. I concluded at a young age that it could happen to me, and it could happen with little or no notice. Kind of like getting lost at an amusement park or being dropped off on a corner far from home. I had a deep and abiding sense that without notice or warning I would be separated and alone in my life, and this belief shaped the way I approached relationships for the next many decades.

What do you think I would tell myself if I could go back? I think I would explain to that young boy that his parents loved him and that he didn't need to feel so insecure. I would tell him that people will try their best but still mess up. I would tell him that he will fail sometimes too; he will just find new and different ways to do it. I would remind him to be for his kids what he needed from others. And I would confirm for him that God will never leave or reject him.

———

Be honest with yourself. Some of the stories we hold on to are holding us back. Let me tell you a quick story about when a young man called me recently to ask for some help. Here's how the conversation went.

"Hey, Bob, I'm trying to figure out what my next career should be. I want to make a change but feel stuck."

"Well, tell me a little bit about what you think you're capable of doing," I said.

"Well, I've actually never really thought about it. Up until now, I kind of just started in my last job when I was young and kept doing it until I decided I needed a change."

To get some big thinking underway, I asked, "Have you ever thought about climbing Mount Rainier?" This incredible mountain is close to where he lived.

"There's no way I could do that," he said. "You see, I experienced a traumatic brain injury when I was younger, and that kind of thing is off-limits for me."

"Oh man, that sounds awful. I'm really sorry to hear that." I wondered what had happened, but I didn't want to pry. "You seem to enjoy talking to people," I said, changing the subject. "I can tell

from this conversation you're pretty good at it. Have you ever considered public speaking?"

"Oh, I could never do that. I had that traumatic brain injury,
remember?"

I could see a pattern forming, so I went rapid-fire to test my
theory.

"What about being a paralegal?"

"Brain injury."

"Pogo-stick jumping?"

"Brain injury."

"Synchronized swimming?"

"Brain injury."

"Spinning a sign at the street corner?"

"Brain injury."

I'm exaggerating a smidge, but you get the idea. He had told
himself a story at a young age that became *the* dominating narrative
of his entire life. Understand me clearly: This isn't just *his* problem.
It's *our* problem. We have an experience, a setback, or a disappointment, and if it isn't understood in a healthy way, it can become a
tsunami in our past that washes farther inland than it should.

I asked my new friend if he would be up for being part of an
experiment. I asked him to try to go an entire day without telling
anyone, even once, that he had experienced a traumatic brain injury
when he was young. Then, try going a week and then a month without telling this factually accurate but functionally debilitating story
and see if the narrative had less control over him. I'm not advocating
living in denial; rather, I'm saying I want to take back some of the
stories, even the true ones that might be hurting our forward progress. What would happen for us if we did the same?

We have a dock behind our house in San Diego. I walked out to
the end of it one evening and noticed a school of minnows making

quite a racket on the surface of the water. It was like ten thousand raindrops falling in a thirty-foot circle. I marveled at how many minnows had made their way to the surface. Then it occurred to me there were probably some big fish underneath that the minnows were trying to get away from. They were being driven to the shallows by the threat of what was underneath. If we want to eliminate some of the distractions in our lives, we need to figure out what or who is chasing us into the shallows.

Your heart and mind are an ocean of endless possibility and promise. We all come into the world with innate personality traits. Unfortunately, we don't get to choose them, or I would have chosen to be a comedian-president-astronaut-country-western-singer and trapeze artist. We also don't get to choose the half-truths or outright lies that the people closest to us believe and espouse. But that's only the case when we're young. You and I have got some life experience now, some miles on the odometer, and quite a few trips around the sun. As a result, you are perfectly positioned to sift through the story of your life to find the origins of who you are. You get to set the course for who you want to be. Don't get distracted by the stories painted on your family history. Don't miss the chance to meet the real. Don't get tricked into being a puddle when your life was meant to be lived as deep as the ocean.

CHAPTER 17

"OH MY GOSH!"

If people are uncomfortable because of your boldness, you're on the right track.

There's a theory called Occam's razor. There's a lot to it, but in essence it says this: The simplest explanation is usually the correct one. Instead of becoming distracted by all the things going on around us and the complicated story plots we assemble in our minds, try going with the simplest explanation. It's usually the right one. Have some of the people you are in relationships with become distractions? Does it bug you that your date always arrives late? Go with the simplest explanation. Maybe their watch is ten minutes off. Does your friend constantly interrupt you? Maybe your friend's hearing is failing. Don't let this become a distraction or an obsession. Think of this as a hall pass. The simplest explanation *isn't* that your date doesn't care about you much anymore, and their lack of punctuality isn't a reflection of their lack of respect for you.

I was in Uganda with my friend Gregg. We were staying in

a little structure out in the bush, and both of us had turned in early, beat from a long time of traversing the country. A few hours later, I woke up to Gregg snoring. He was really sawing logs, and truly horrific sounds were coming out of him while he slept. It was simply unnatural. I lay in bed for hours staring at the ceiling, listening to the unrelenting din of his snoring as it rattled the nails loose in the roof and shook the windows. If I'd had a Taser, I would have used it on him. In my exhaustion, I wondered how much trouble I would be in if I put a pillow over his head and took him out. It seemed on the one hand like it might be an act of kindness to assist him in shuffling off this mortal coil. *Besides, I have diplomatic immunity*, I thought. I wondered if it would hold up in court. *Or perhaps I could lean on a self-defense appeal. Who knows? Life in prison is less and less of a disincentive for a guy like me who is already in his sixties.* These were the musings of a frustrated, sleep-deprived man.

I was quoting *Hamlet* to myself at 2:00 a.m. and still had not slept a wink. Mercifully the sun rose a few hours later, and I stumbled into the main room where Gregg was already up. I walked in and gave him my most incredulous, gunslinger stare. "Dude, you need an operation or something. I've never heard anyone snore like you. I've never even heard a story about a guy who snores as loud as you." Gregg looked up a little surprised and provoked and said, "Me? Bob, I've never heard anyone snore as loud as *you*. I didn't sleep a minute all night. That's why I'm up."

Wait, what? I never slept; how could I be snoring? Unconvinced, the two of us were still pointing fingers at each other's noses and searching for metaphors about how loud the other guy had been snoring the night before as we walked out the front door to sit on the porch. Just then, that horrible, groaning, rumbling, snoring sound surrounded both of us. We followed the sounds around to the back of the hut. There we found a huge cow who had been up all night giving birth to a calf.

Remember Occam's razor. Don't be too hard on each other. Things aren't always the way they appear or even what they sound like.

———————

You are going to be misunderstood, and you will misunderstand some things. It's just that simple. It's going to happen all day, every day, and twice on Sundays—maybe three times if you speak at a church, have a teenager, or are a teenager. You won't even understand yourself sometimes, which is crazy because you are always with you. You'll misunderstand others too. Not just once in a while, either, but constantly. If you're not aware that this has been happening, you have misunderstood yet another thing. Having predictable disconnects and miscues is like having a chive stuck in your front tooth. Everyone else knows, but you haven't figured it out yet.

I could tell you about the five ways we each communicate and how we could do a better job at it, or three techniques for listening and increasing the clarity of our communications. As an alternative, what if we just blow past all that and instead get more comfortable with people just not "getting us" and stop getting distracted when this occurs? For some people, this proposition is simply unthinkable. When another misunderstanding occurs, it sucks all the air out of the room. Is this you? If it is, I've got two helpful words for you. *Stop it.*

Obsessing over predictable misunderstandings distracts everyone around you as you flail around trying to clarify everything. What if we come up with a strategy in advance, instead of dealing with being misunderstood? There is a chance you will experience freedom from this persistent problem and constant source of distraction.

Get comfortable with the notion that some people will be puzzled by what you say and do. Rather than being distracted by this, just admit it, understand it, and grow through it. Stop sweating it, regretting it, looking over your shoulder, replaying old conversations in your mind, and hoping for a different outcome. Once we blow the foam off the top, what is often most painful about being misunderstood is the deeper challenge that has been made to our underlying motives or intentions or values. Don't get punked by these challenges; understand the nature and inevitability of misunderstanding, and you will gut all the power it has over you.

Following Jesus means being constantly misunderstood. Sure, it hurts. No one seeks it out, enjoys feeling attacked, or appreciates being raked over the coals. The truth is, misunderstanding often leads to disconnection. The people who don't "get you anymore" will probably find a way to create some distance between them and you. Don't be discouraged if that happens to you. They killed Jesus when He was misunderstood, so what's a bad day for you? Jesus was talking to His Father and told Him that He had brought honor to God by finishing the work He had been given.[1] What if you tap the brakes on all the distractions and finish the work you've been given rather than worrying about how everyone feels about what you're doing?

If finishing the work God gave you rubs somebody wrong, you'll probably be dropped from a couple of email groups or be uninvited from a gathering or two. Big deal. Let these disappointments roll off like water off a duck's back. You don't need thicker skin; you need more awareness and perspective and an unwavering sense of purpose. Don't get me wrong; I'm not saying we should aim for being misunderstood, but maybe, just maybe, we could stop obsessing over it when it happens again.

I have never been very good at figuring out what things cost. I go to the store and still think I can get a pair of blue jeans for six bucks. Some of the ones they sell these days look like they went nine rounds with a raccoon and are selling for hundreds, just because they're all torn up and ripped. I just don't get it.

With our work at The Oaks, I needed something a little more stout to carry the horse and cattle trailers and hay. A Prius just isn't going to cut it. I went to the car dealership and found a pickup truck with rubber mats instead of carpet. It was pretty stripped down, so I figured I could afford it and asked the guy to write it up. When he told me the cost, I did a double take. This was twice what I had paid for my entire college education.

I got on the want ads and found a used truck with one hundred thousand miles on it and met the young guy selling it for cheap. It was just what I was looking for, and I drove away. On the way home I smelled a strong soap smell but dismissed it as a passing thing. I have a friend with a nose like a beagle, but I've never had a very sensitive olfactory sense. Sure, I can pick up on smells if someone doused themselves with perfume or dollar cologne, or let one rip in an elevator, but otherwise I don't give smells much thought. I rolled down the windows of the truck, thinking I could just air out the cab of my new-old truck on the drive home. One last sniff when I got to the curb at home, and it smelled like I had nailed it and the odor was gone.

The next morning I got back in the truck to run an errand, and when I opened the door that same strong smell of soap came pouring out like bubbles from an overfilled washing machine. I had to drive several hours up to Los Angeles for a wedding, and the soapy smell was really starting to bug me. I figured if I couldn't blow it out with the windows open, I'd cook it out. I turned the heater to max, and for the next three hours up to Los Angeles and three hours back home, I tried to burn the soapy scent away. I pitted out my shirt in the process but was satisfied when I got home that I'd knocked out the problem. One last sniff again to confirm I had been the victor in the battle of the smells when I got home—and I as I suspected, I was certain I had crushed it. I had been truly victorious. The smell had represented all things wrong with the world, but I was the equivalent of a baking soda warrior and this distraction had crumbled at my feet.

The next morning when I got back in the truck, I opened the door to the same soap smell all over again. Have you ever gotten so locked onto something that you temporary lose your mind? I mean totally rubber-room lose it, completely and irrationally fixating on something that shouldn't matter that much? This is exactly what happened to me, and somehow I found myself at the auto upholstery store. I tossed the keys to my soapy truck on the counter and told them to replace the entire interior of the truck with leather seats, carpet, the works. I might as well be comfortable if I have to get rid of the smell, right? Three days later I picked up the truck and opened the door. It smelled like dead cow—and soap. *Nooo!*

I got in the truck with my head hung low and nose plugged. I reached up above to put my sunglasses in the tray hanging from the ceiling, and as I did I felt something lodged in the compartment. I pulled it down and found a twenty-five-cent air freshener shaped like a bar of soap. I realized in that moment I had spent two thousand dollars fixing a twenty-five-cent problem. When an unreasonable amount of attention is given to a distraction, it can become an obsession. We can obsess over all kinds of things. Sports, people's opinions about us, politics, even air fresheners. Here are my questions to you: What are you obsessing over? Is it a relationship? An opportunity? A job? A failure? Whatever it is, these obsessions are not doing you any favors. Remember, Occam's razor. Go with the simplest explanation.

I was in London speaking at a gathering for a large church. They meet for church in the West End of the city in a theater that is packed all week with stage performances. Each Sunday morning, they change the place into a church, and people line up for hours just to get inside. The stage had all the props for whatever stage play was showing when I arrived, and it must have been a good one because it looked otherworldly with lava covering a stage that sloped sharply toward the audience. When I get a chance to speak to a lot of people, I like to stand right on the edge of the stage with my feet hanging over. It feels sportier that way, and I like knowing that if I lose my balance and fall into the orchestra pit, I'll end up in a kettledrum.

This particular Sunday, there was a line of people waiting to get into the theater that wrapped around four city blocks. It would be a couple of hours before we started the service, and since I'm not a guy who wants to hang out in the greenroom and eat Twinkies, I went out and started giving hugs and welcoming everyone in line to church. "I'm so glad you're here! It's going to be a great morning!" I told each waiting person, waving my arms in the air before wrapping them in a noncreepy hug. About sixty minutes later, the guy in front of me had a tweed jacket on, and I gave him a huge hug like I had to everyone else. "Welcome!" I said. "This is going to be a terrific day. I'm so glad you came to church!" He looked a little surprised, frozen in place like a statue when I gave him the big welcome hug. I figured out why a few minutes later. It turns out that the line had ended thirty yards earlier, and he was just a British guy walking down the street in London when the crazy American ran up and gave him an overly enthusiastic hug. He was probably thinking to himself he was glad my ancestors had boarded a ship, sailed across the ocean, and made their own country. Just like you will miss a couple of things along the way and not get them right, you're going to be misunderstood. Deal with it, own it, embrace it, hug it. Don't be distracted by it.

Our faith communities are wonderfully diverse in expression. Some wave their hands in the air and make a lot of noise, while others wear robes and keep their arms at their sides. Some hold their palms up, and others press their palms together. Some sing hymns with a choir and have cello ensembles and responsive readings, and still others crowd-surf, play contemporary music, and rock the house while smoke machines pump in the vibe. You don't need to identify with all of it to appreciate it. Don't get distracted when someone else connects with God in a way that wouldn't have any sway with you. The same holds true with the way someone describes their experience with God. Being one in God doesn't mean we need to be the same.

Someone asked me if I was watering down the gospel in the books I write. "Actually," I said, "I hope so." Here's why. I want to write books for thirsty people. There's a lot of people who are full of opinions but parched in their own lives because they simply aren't thirsty anymore. Be among the thirsty ones, and you will remain undistracted when someone describes their journey in a way that is different from how you would describe yours. Don't just know the Scriptures but delight in the freedom they can bring you if you are willing. As Sweet Maria tells me all the time: Keep your eyes on your own paper.

I'm a lawyer, so I pick juries. Doing this requires that I size up in a hurry the people who are prospective jurors. Morticians do the same and size people quickly too. What if we stopped sizing each other up? Instead, if we were to tend to our own fires, perhaps they would burn a little brighter. We need to stop getting into food fights with people inside and outside of our faith communities just because we don't understand or agree with their worldview. Remember, God didn't appoint us judge and jury just because we have a couple of opinions. Do us a favor and keep divisive thoughts to yourself. Instead, delight in how wonderfully diverse we are.

Remember, we are supposed to be love's heroes, not its bouncers. Sadly, some of us have become so distracted trying to straighten everybody else out that we have swerved off the road. It turns out that most of pride's prisoners actually think they're the guards. Don't become one of them. I'm not saying go light on sound doctrine. I am saying if we go big on Jesus, we'll be living out some great theology.

I spoke at an event in Texas. We had a terrific time together, and the next day I received a telephone call from a woman. "Hi, I was at the event you spoke at last night," she said.

"Terrific! How did you like it?" I asked.

"Oh, I hated it!"

"You hated my talk? Which part?"

"The whole thing."

"Oh my gosh," I stammered, wondering what I had said that had been so off-putting. "How come?"

She said, "You were cussing the whole time."

I thought about it for a second and didn't remember having accidentally dropped any f-bombs.

"What in the world did I say that offended you?"

She snapped back, "You said 'oh my gosh' a couple of times."

"Oh my gosh," I said, holding back a laugh. She must have thought I had Tourette's. This phrase just wasn't a cuss word to me. We obviously hadn't gone to the same high school.

I had been misunderstood yet again. I invited her to have a Slurpee with me next time I was in town, then wondered which poor sap she'd be calling next on her list of strangers she felt it was her job to dress down. When you're tempted to call out strangers about things they've said, why not make the call from the local Red Cross as you're giving a pint of blood to someone in need or while you're changing someone's flat tire on the side of the road? We can distract ourselves thinking that we're giving people needed advice on how to live their lives without actually adding anything to their lives. Know what I mean?

You are going to be misunderstood. You will mess up more than a couple of things and get still more wrong. It's not going to happen once in a while. It will happen constantly. So figure out in advance what you'll do when it happens next, and oh my gosh (I couldn't resist), the freedom you gain will be worth it.

CHAPTER 18

FIVE MINUTES FROM NOW

*The work you do is not a way to
prove your worth; it is proof that God
already sees you as worthwhile.*

One time I flew into a city in the South for a speaking event, and a
really nice guy told me he would come to the airport to fetch me.
I'm terrible at directions, so I'm always grateful for a ride. I walked
out of the airport and up to his unassuming car at the curb outside
of the baggage claim. Inside was an older guy with a warm smile
and a firm handshake. It was the middle of the day, so I assumed he
was retired and was just willing to do me a solid by giving me a lift.

I got in his car and thanked him for the ride, and he told me he
was always happy to help out. I could tell that hospitality came easy
to him. We got on the highway, and he began to tell me a story about
his family and how they went on a trip to Washington DC when he
was young. He recalled that his family, which included a number of
siblings, checked into a hotel with his parents when they arrived in

the capital decades ago. I was thinking to myself as he spoke, *This is going to be a pretty long story*, but hey, I had all day, and he was a nice guy, so I asked a few more questions. He told me the hotel his family checked into was frayed around the edges and inexpensive. And when his father checked out, the clerk said it would cost one dollar extra for each kid. His dad was furious that this hotel would tack on a charge for the children, and the whole drive home from the trip his father was incensed and grumbling about it.

My driver said his father decided by the time they got home that this hotel was just wrong and something needed to be done about it.

We pulled into the hotel where I would spend the night as my new friend wrapped up his story. In an unusually kind gesture, he didn't just drop me off but got out of the car and walked with me across the parking lot and into the lobby. One of the hotel workers passed us in the lobby and greeted my driver. "Hi, Mr. Wilson." *Funny, maybe he comes here often*, I thought to myself. I got to the front desk to check in, and the clerk looked up at me and my friend and said, "Oh, hi, Mr. Wilson!" in a cheery voice. Huh? He knew the front desk clerk too? He was a nice guy, but I doubted he stayed at the hotel often since he lived in the city. I turned to my driver. "Mr. Wilson, do you come here often?" He just shrugged it off and smiled warmly. As he did, another person passed by and said, "Hey, Mr. Wilson!" I was wondering if there was a hidden camera somewhere and I was the only one who didn't get the prank being played on me.

"Okay, okay," I said to my new friend, "what's the deal?"

He gave a gentle grin and said, "Well"—he paused for a long second—"it's my hotel."

"You own this Holiday Inn?"

"Well," and then another grin, "actually, all of them, in a way."

It turns out my unassuming driver was the son of Kemmons

Wilson, who, when he and his family returned from their trip to Washington DC, decided to start his own hotel chain. One of the original architects of the first hotels had evidently joked about a movie named *Holiday Inn* while they were doing some late-night planning, and the rest is history.

Faith was important to Kemmons and his partner, so they put a Bible in every room—which was a first. He opened the flagship Holiday Inn in Memphis in the late 1950s, and the one-thousandth Holiday Inn opened in the late 1960s. Then they kept building more. What a story.

Here's my point. Many of us become distracted trying to look important. My driver, Mr. Wilson, didn't. He was important, but it wasn't because his family owned a successful hotel chain. He was important because he was known and loved by God. You are too. He reflected his importance in the way he honored and respected the people who worked for him with a quiet, confident humility and the way he made time for wayward travelers like me. It's been said that there are two kinds of people: humble people and those about to be. Be humble and you won't be distracted trying to look important.

———

Do you remember the last time you mingled with some new people? Maybe it was a backyard barbecue or waiting your turn for a parent-teacher conference. Maybe it was at a book club or at the oil change center or your first time in a new Sunday school group or at a baby shower. What is the most common question asked in settings where new acquaintances are learning about each other? If your experience is anything like mine, that question is: *What do you do?* Meaning, what do you do *for a living*?

We are hardwired to ask this question because we have collectively agreed that work is important and might leave some clues about what is central to our lives. It's the way we feed our families or our egos. It's how we pay the bills or comply with people's expectations. Work takes up the lion's share of our days. In fact, on average, humans will spend 30 percent of their life working. The only thing we spend more time on is sleeping, only by a few percentage points.

The subtle twist that happens with work, though, compared to our other daily activities, is that it's easy to conflate *what we do* with *who we are.* In other words, we equate our work with our worth and identity. This is where things can get tricky and dangerous and confusing. Besides, it's easier to ask people *What do you do?* rather than *Who are you?* We are concerned about going too deep too fast, so we ask less-personal questions like, *What team are you rooting for?* rather than *How much sleep do you get every night?* I get it. It can come off as creepy if you ask deep questions without a relationship to back up the gesture.

Here's a different question I think is worth asking: How much are you relying on your job for your identity? Is your work your calling card, the thing you're proud to talk about at dinner parties? Maybe your work is the expression of dutifully following other people's expectations. *My grandpa and my dad were both in the army, so I felt like I should follow in their footsteps.* Or maybe this sounds more familiar: *I really wanted to be a [musician, chef, therapist, veterinarian, entrepreneur, stockbroker, teacher, drummer], but my parents discouraged it.*

If we are to become less distracted, we need to get a better, healthier handle on our work and the position God meant for it to hold in our lives. But that can be utterly confusing, right? We're trying to figure this stuff out midstride, midjob, midcareer, and we

FIVE MINUTES FROM NOW

feel tethered to the thing we are currently doing even though it may not be working for us anymore.

I used to go to this restaurant and often got the same server. He was young, energetic, full of ambition, and using the job to earn the money he needed for the direction he was headed. I went there again recently, nearly ten years later, and guess who was still there? He remembered me, and I recalled those plans he mentioned all those years ago. He said, "Oh yeah. I really wanted to do that, but the money here was too good, and I needed to pay my bills." In the past he practically beamed with purpose as he zipped around the restaurant—knowing what he was working toward. Now he seemed grizzled and tired, shoulders slumping, and going through the motions as he took my order. Life can be tough, and it throws us a few curveballs sometimes—but I wondered if he'd stopped working toward something and now merely worked somewhere instead, and the choice was clearly not doing him any favors.

Don't get me wrong. The undistracted people I know work their tails off. They know their purposes and are relentless and joyful in their pursuit of them. Some have lots of money; some of them don't. Some of these friends work in jobs that would seem glamorous to the rest of us; some get immense satisfaction from jobs we would never take in a million years. The point is this: What we do matters less than what we are working toward, who we're working for, and why we are doing it. Think about this and apply it to yourself for a second. What would you change?

Did you know that Paul in the Bible said we should work as if God is our boss?[1] I like this perspective. God wants us to view our work as a way to honor Him, get closer to Him, and reflect Him in how we live. Think about the first thing we see God doing in the Bible in the book of Genesis. He's working. He's creating. He's building out a vision for the universe and then hovering over it, evaluating the beauty of what He did. It's mysterious and wonderful to think that of all the things God made, we are the crown jewels. Do you think God wants us to toil meaninglessly in our work? Of course not. He wants us to reflect pieces of Him in whatever we create and do. We can do this by bagging groceries or landing on the moon. Whenever we are creating through our acts of work—and whenever we work as if God is the real boss—we are on the right track. It doesn't matter what the work is; it matters who we become in the process of doing our work, and the goal is to look and act more like Jesus while we do it.

If God imbued us with this desire to work, and if we shape our identities around this time-consuming aspect of life, shaking the apple cart can feel like a soul-level risk. It can feel like we are standing on the end of the high dive absolutely frozen and unable to jump. If this sounds like you, my word for you is as simple as it is difficult: Make the jump. If nothing else, you will make a daring leap toward who you are becoming and what you are working toward, and that's better than a decade stuck waiting tables when the job isn't for you anymore.

———

Some of us make big plans and big commitments for the future. It's not wrong to plan or commit, but the truth is, most of us are just guessing what the next hour will hold. I want people to work with me because it's the right thing right now, not because it was the right thing a year ago. People are supposed to change. Get real about it when they do and you do. Encourage change. Respectfully demand it of the people you work with and of yourself. It's not disloyal to change. It's irreverent not to. Most of us are a job or two behind who we have become. That's not a bad thing. In fact, it's a good thing. It means we are changing. Our interests are evolving, and our capabilities are constantly expanding if we are doing life correctly.

I had been going year to year with my day job as a lawyer for a couple of decades, and it worked out really well. At some point, however, I decided I had changed so much from who I once was that being a lawyer had become a distraction, so I quit. I didn't plan on it, think about it more, or worry about it. I simply quit. Like Cortez, I burned the ships. Most people pick their careers and backfill their lives with any space left over. Sweet Maria and I decided we would pick our lives first, then backfill our careers behind them. A few of my good ideas have worked, and a few bad ones have worked too. Some ideas I thought were really terrific didn't come together. I used to spend my time doing things that worked. Now I'm trying to do things that last. It's a subtle difference but an important one.

One of the mistakes I made early on was doing the things I was *able* to do. I'll give you an example. I'm able to play the banjo. I'm no Earl Scruggs. If you heard me hack my way through his famous "Foggy Mountain Breakdown," you would know that. What I'm doing now is finding the things I'm made to do and doing lots of that. Swapping "able to" to "made to" involves constant change, a clear understanding of purpose, and undistracted, unwavering resolve to do what it takes to get there. Not knowing how to do something doesn't need to slow you down; let it speed you up. Finding what we are made to do means trying lots of things. I'm buying a set of bagpipes. No lie. Get a set for yourself. You'll look great in a kilt. It's okay to try out a few things and then ditch them when they're not giving you the right feedback signal.

Bad jobs make volunteering more attractive and make college and grad school look more enticing. Bad bosses make us better employers. Lousy job duties make us more compassionate and sensitive to the people who took our places. These bad jobs refine our worldview and remind us about what's meaningful. Most people don't want better careers; they want more purpose. Here's the great news: God said purpose is available by the barrel.

Find a job that suits you, one that doesn't conflict with the life you want and the life you want for those you love. I'm not smart enough to be a doctor, but if I were, I wouldn't be a dermatologist because I would need to be where the pimple or rash was. I want a lot of freedom. To the contrary, others find comfort in structure. If you don't like blood, you shouldn't work for the Red Cross. If you don't like numbers, don't become an accountant. If you can't handle conflict, don't be a lawyer. If you don't want to draw a lot of attention to yourself, don't be a pastor.

Pick where you want to live. Don't let your job pick the place you will call home. I live in San Diego, but I worked in Seattle for a quarter of a century. Most days, I would get on a plane early in the morning, fly to Seattle, and be home for dinner. Our kids were in junior high before they figured out I worked at the other end of the country. "Dad, you said you worked downtown," they said over dinner one night.

"I do," I said with a grin.

Before I owned my own law firm, I was a partner at someone else's. When our kids were young, the days were pretty simple: Keep them mostly fed and clothed, keep their hands off the stove, and keep the goldfish in the bowl. As they got bigger and learned how to walk and talk, things got pretty interesting. I wanted to talk to them more because they could talk to me and I could get into mischief with them. I wanted to hang out with them, and they wanted to spend time with me. So one Friday in the early summer I told twenty of my law partners that I was going to spend the next few months with my family at our place in Canada. They looked at me like I was carrying a yellow umbrella and wearing snowshoes. They shook their heads in unison and reminded me how the sabbatical program worked. After ten years, I'd get fifteen minutes off.

I didn't argue with them. On Monday, I just wasn't there; I was in Canada with my family. I'm not kidding. A couple of months later, I came back. I couldn't imagine any group of guys more bent out of shape, until the next summer when I did the same thing. Was it irresponsible? Maybe. But it would have been worse to miss out on the lives of my terrific family.

Listen, I need my family and you need yours. It's easy to spend so much time providing for your family that you're no longer providing for your family. Do you get me? Don't wait until later to connect with your families. It won't happen. Choose your family over and over, and you know what? When you're older, they'll choose you back.

Some people do a great job in the marketplace, and some do a great job with their families. The trick is to do both. Do lots of things. Do risky things. I've burned my eyebrows off more than a couple of times by mistake. Do meaningful things, selfless things. Find ways to shape your family's hearts, and you won't need a slogan. Take all the goodness and beauty and freedom you experience back to the work you do. When people ask my kids what I do for a living, they just laugh and walk away. It's probably because we're all still trying to figure out what it is.

You know those little sticks of honey you can get at the coffee shop for your tea? That is the life's work of about a dozen bees. People who are focused on their purpose don't want to rule the hive; they want to put their quarter inch of honey on top of everyone else's and participate in making something lasting. Even the honey buried with the pharaohs is still sweet. This is the kind of shelf life I'm looking for when it comes to the things I throw my weight into. Purpose and joy will go the distance every time; distraction won't get you to the end of the week.

If you want to uncover the things that will *last* in your life, get rid of the distractions that should be the *least* in your life. Stay eager to know or learn something new every day. People who change the world may have many similar personality traits, but they all seem to have one thing in common: They're curious about everything. Most of us don't know how a zipper works, how a violin string makes sound, or why corn pops. Don't settle for just clothing and feeding yourself each day and calling it a life. Go learn something new, and you'll find a new gear for living.

Some people go through life looking lost and hopeless and older than their chronological ages. Maybe they just stopped being curious and it affected the way they look and feel and live. Don't be one of them. Most of all, stay curious about the people you love most. Engage with them in such a way that they, too, will want to find their purpose while you are finding yours. It will be the most beautiful journey you can share with them.

It's going to take some time and effort to get clarity on what you are working toward. You may have spent ten years thinking about your next move and are now feeling scared or stuck. Maybe you have only been thinking about it for the last ten minutes while reading this chapter. Perhaps you need to get out of your head and get busy doing something. What are you waiting for?

I get it. Sometimes life's circumstances feel like the sock drawer just got thrown on the floor. It's a mess to be sure, but what a great time to start untangling the argyle sock that's been balled up with the gym sock and find a better match. It only took one year and forty-five days to build the Empire State Building. Don't put it on a list or wait another year; get busy right now building what the rest of your life will look like. I know you want to plan it all out—me, too, sometimes—but remember this: The builders of the Empire State Building were on the thirtieth floor building while they were still working out the details for the first floor.

Your life is a building. You can change what gets constructed as the floors go higher and higher. You don't have to be who you were five years ago or even five minutes ago. You have coagency with God to decide who you will be five years from now, and it starts with what you do five minutes from now. If you want to live a life of purpose and joy and less distraction, it will likely take some new schematics. Nobody gets it right the first try. Trust me. Just remember that the moment you stop working toward something, the building project has stopped. Let's stop living as if the project is done and get back to the business of reconstructing our life and the lives of those we love back up to the sky.

CHAPTER 19

FINISH YOUR WORK

If you want to honor and dazzle God,
find the work He has given you,
and do it until the job is done.

When I was in college, I met a guy who made guitars. I lived in Northern California in a small beach city called Arcadia. People there smoked a lot, but not cigarettes. Jim had a little shop in town not far from campus with a small window facing the sidewalk. He had long hair and a beard, wore lots of ceramic beads around his neck, and always rocked a faded blue-denim jacket and pair of suede desert boots with gum soles. Each week I would put my nose up against the window, peer inside, and delight in seeing wood shavings, tools, and a stringed instrument another step closer to completion. I remembered my days in high school woodshop and all the life lessons I had learned there.

Becoming a luthier isn't easy. It's like getting a PhD in wood-working and takes years of practice, patience, and a deep love for creating. It also requires the right tools and the ability to see the finished product in the raw wood and somehow hear the music it could make someday. This isn't easy for some of us to do with our lives. We may have a couple of pieces, and perhaps we even have a few of the tools needed to create a beautiful life. But we often lack the knowledge or experience or instruction to finish the work Paul said God had started inside of us a long time ago.

One day I decided to walk into Jim's humble store and tentatively pushed open the squeaky door. Over my head, a small, old-school bell jingled, giving me away. Jim looked up from the instrument he was working on, a little surprised to have someone inside his shop. I guess it didn't happen often. I introduced myself and asked if he would teach me how to make a guitar. "You bet," he nonchalantly chirped, briefly looking up from the instrument he was working on.

I had practiced my pitch for why I would be a good investment of his time. I had planned to tell him how I was pretty good at playing the guitar, and I was a nice guy, and once I'd even had a puppy. I convinced myself it would take a great deal of advocacy to get what I wanted, and it probably wouldn't happen in the end. I thought it would be a big imposition, and I had already prepared myself to be turned down flat. When Jim gave an immediate and unequivocal green light, I didn't know what to say. "Really?" just sort of dribbled out. I failed to find anything better deep in my reservoir of energetic responses to this kind of extravagant kindness.

"Sure," he said. "Come back later this week and we'll get started." I skipped out of the shop dreaming about tools and wood shavings and guitar shredding and what a cool accomplishment it would be to *build my own guitar.*

When I arrived at his shop a few days later, he had placed a couple of mahogany and spruce boards on the table. He told me we would run them through the planer and make them thin enough for the guitar sides and back. Then we used another larger piece to shape the guitar neck. Once we had done this, we built a form out of pine in the outline of a guitar body with all of the curves.

The next week, to make them pliable, we soaked the thin wood pieces we had planed, bent them around the form we had built, and securely clamped them to permanently take on the shape of the mold. Weeks later, we added a supporting brace, affixed the back of the guitar, and put spruce on top after I cut a sound hole. After that process was complete, I made a saddle where the strings would attach and sanded small pieces of wood to make bridge pins to hold the strings in place. Then Jim showed me how to shape the neck and headstock. I was just about finished. All told this took about six months, which flew by in a blink. Jim and I became pretty good friends in the process. There was only one last thing to do to finish the guitar: I needed to make a fretboard.

Every time I left the shop, I imagined my fingers dancing up and down the carefully carved neck, landing perfectly on the frets, while I melted hearts with the music coming out of my handmade guitar. I was so excited to complete this project and planned to skip some of my last week of classes to finish this final step.

Unfortunately, Jim was out sick for the week. A huge bummer, but I was undeterred. Then I got what he got, and that put me back another week or so. Anyone who knows me well knows that when I get sick, I nosedive pretty fast. I spent that sick time moaning and groaning in a dark room with the world completely shut out. In that sad state, the last day of classes at the university happened too. Just as I was recovering, we all got kicked out of the dorms for the summer. I don't remember taking my finals but somehow passed anyway.

I tried Jim's store a few more times, but my timing seemed cursed. He wasn't there day after day. I eventually realized I would have to become a homeless luthier or find somewhere I could get a job and pay the rent. So I moved to Southern California, got a job, and scrounged up enough to buy a surfboard. I never got around to finishing the fretboard to complete the guitar. I got *distracted*.

Not long ago, I was up in our attic and came across an old guitar case. I wondered which of my three grown children had left it behind. I opened the case and inside was a wooden guitar with no fretboard. I had completely forgotten about it. I started counting on my fingers and toes and realized this unfinished guitar was forty-two years old. Where had the time gone? It was like I was Rip Van Winkle and had fallen asleep, grown a foot-long beard, gotten married, made three people, and had a couple of careers. I had started making that guitar with so much enthusiasm and was so close to finishing, but I stalled out. It wasn't that the guitar was unimportant to me. It was the slow drift of other things getting in the way. This happens to all of us in different ways. Distractions come in the form of a job, a relationship, a school, a move, a couple of kids, a 401(k). It's not conscious deferral; it's the mission-creep we succumb to.

I pulled the dusty guitar case down from the attic and put it by the front door to be a daily reminder. I don't have forty-two years left in me, and I didn't want to be distracted anymore. The next day I started my search for someone to help me finish the fretboard. I found a guy named Jed. He looked like he used to play for the Doobie Brothers and reminded me of the guy who helped me start this project decades earlier. Jed started repairing guitars when I began crafting mine, and, like me, he was now an old guy. I brought the guitar into his shop, and he took a look at the unfinished instrument in the case. He pulled it out by the neck and said, "Dude, not bad. You were so close to being done."

"Yeah, I know," I said. In the past, I probably would've run through all the excuses for why I didn't finish and sprinkle it with a little self-shaming. But I was encouraged by his optimism. Something had changed in me over the years and I wasn't ashamed of what was left undone. Instead, I rediscovered my original dream and reignited my desire to finish. I had just needed someone to help me get there.

Jesus was talking to His Father one day, and He let us eavesdrop on the conversation. He said He had brought glory and honor to His Father by finishing the work He had been given to do. I can understand that kind of theology. If you want to honor God like Jesus did, finish what He gave you to do. Do you have a song yet to be written? *Finish your work.* Do you have a book inside of you, but you've been deferring the process of writing? *Pick up your pen.* Do you have a strained relationship that demands a difficult conversation? *Make the call.* Are you stuck in a job that isn't you anymore? *Quit.* Literally, finish your work. Or is there someone you have wanted to connect with but have felt like it would be too big of a risk to ask? Don't just start the work like I did with my guitar; finish it.

You might need to find someone to help you take the last courageous step. Find a safe friend, a wise counselor, a family member, a trustworthy pastor, or the guy at the tire store. Seek out people who have the patience and experience or the deep love for creating that you may lack. Identify people who get things done and draw close to them. Figure out what has been getting in the way, those things that have been distracting you, and eliminate them. If you want to honor and dazzle God, find the work He has given you, and do it until the job is done.

I arrived at the San Diego International Airport, headed to another city for a speaking engagement. I am constantly in the terminal on my way either to a speaking event or on the way back from one. The ticket agents behind the counters are my people. I have had them over to the house, and we have celebrated birthdays, graduations, and other important dates together. I have helped a few of them with international adoptions and a handful of others with car or roommate problems. They call me "Mr. G" when I arrive and often put a ticket on the counter for me to grab as I whisk by. This day I knew I would be pinched for time once I got to the airport. I don't normally like the rush, but I'd planned to run late and give myself the extra time I wanted with Sweet Maria before dashing away again. It was a good trade. Besides, I hadn't missed a flight for a speaking event in years.

I made it through security quickly, which wasn't a surprise. Just like at the ticket counter, it's a class reunion most days at the TSA machines. When I walk through the metal detector, I usually forget to remove my Mickey Mouse watch and get directed to the left for the more invasive full body search. I awkwardly smile at these familiar faces and turn my pockets inside out as they wave wands around me and rifle through my backpack full of partially written books, Rubik's Cubes, saltwater taffy, and various props for the next talk.

Once through security, I hurried to the gate knowing I was running pretty late, even for me. Instead of finding the last boarding procedure and hearing my name announced over the loudspeakers, I sensed lethargy at the gate and saw a huge ball of people gathered near the ticket counter. No one was going anywhere. I looked up and down the concourse, and the same was true at every other gate. No one knew what was going on.

Over the airport public address system, a pleasant but remarkably disinterested voice announced that no flights would come into or out of the airport for some time. "A full ground stop has gone into effect while authorities take appropriate safety measures." The neon lights on the arrival and departure board flickered as every flight was canceled and thirty more were diverted to other cities to land. The hubbub in the crowded terminal became as frantic as the blinking lights on the flight boards.

It was a long ten minutes before the truth spread through the terminal about the reason for all the cancellations. To understand the alarm, you need to get a sense of where the San Diego Airport is located. It is wedged between the hills of Balboa Park to the east, skyscrapers in the downtown area to the south, and Point Loma to the west. It is smack-dab in the middle of a dense urban area. The surrounding topography demands that airplanes come in low while still clearing the apartment complexes, high-rises, and stores filled with people below. I have piloted an airplane into Lindbergh Field, and the approach to runway 27 can be tricky for pilots entering the airspace for the first time. It feels as if the wings are grazing the rooftops.

As it turns out, an active shooter with a high-powered rifle was in one of the apartments just east of the airport.

In other words, there was a sniper in the flight path.

I later learned there was a massive standoff that lasted five hours. After many shots were fired, the standoff was as over as the event I was supposed to be attending. I suppose I should have just stayed with Sweet Maria for a few more minutes.

Here's my question for you: Who or what is the sniper in your path? If we can identify the distractions in our lives, we can find a path forward by moving through them, going around them, or walking away from them. It only took one sniper to shut down an entire airport, and this makes sense to us—but what about the distractions you have allowed to shut you down completely? Is it a job or a relationship or a failure that has grounded you? What has this distraction cost you? Your creativity? Your generosity? Your willingness to risk again? Did your desire to dive into vulnerable, authentic relationships take a hit?

Make no mistake. Distractions are being fired in your direction. They come every day in the form of disappointments, insecurities, setbacks, small public failures, or huge private ones. Whatever your snipers, they will likely lurk around in your life and pop up in some related form in the future. Let's not act surprised when this happens; let's be prepared. If we don't figure out a plan in advance, these distractions will wreak havoc in our lives. They have the power to shut us down if we're willing to tolerate or ignore their presence.

―――――

A long time ago a guy named Artaxerxes was the Persian ruler of the Jewish people. Despite some early friction between Artaxerxes and the Jews, he had an unexplained change of heart toward them as a people. Nehemiah was a servant—the king's cupbearer—when all of this was going on. The cupbearer was a special job in the palace. This person would pour the wine and taste it before the king did. It wouldn't have been a bad first job—unless someone was trying to poison the king and you got a mouthful. Then, not so much.

Nehemiah was someone the king trusted with his life, but he was also a slave to him. It was an odd juxtaposition but a deal many of us make all the time. Jerusalem was the big city. If you've read the history books, it was forever in the middle of a controversy, much as it still is. It was leveled twice, attacked more than seventy-five times, and recaptured almost as often. One group would overthrow the city, destroy it, and take over, then another group would arrive and do the same. The last group that overthrew the city of Jerusalem had the city walls destroyed and the gates burned (again).

Nehemiah had a special love for Jerusalem and asked the king if he could leave court and help rebuild the city. It was a bold ask for a slave, but the king trusted him and told him he could take leave and go.

There was a lot of work to do, but Nehemiah didn't just think about it; he got to work. It wasn't long afterward that some people tried to distract him. These men called him names, said mean things about him, and tried to intimidate him. Their hope was that Nehemiah would become so distracted that he would bail on what he had come to do. Nehemiah made a power move I hope you will adopt in your life. He looked down at the men below calling his name and declared: "I'm doing important work, and I can't come down!" He was a guy who had cracked the code. He knew what he was there to do. He knew why he was doing it. And he wouldn't be distracted.

Another group figured out where Nehemiah was and threw everything and the kitchen sink at him to get him off task—but once again it didn't work. Nehemiah yelled down to them while stacking bricks on the wall.

"I'm doing important work, and I can't come down!"

I can see him—head down, focused, confident, unwilling to yield to the noise around him. Nehemiah knew plenty about distractions, including the power of a distraction to interfere with his larger God-given purposes. He knew these distractions would come his way, and he figured out what he was going to say when they did. You should take a lesson from him.

"I'm doing important work, and I can't come down!"

He probably practiced in the mirror so he didn't have to think about it on the spot. Do the same. Practice saying this to disruptions when they come your way.

"I'm doing important work, and I can't come down!"

This phrase wasn't just a slogan for Nehemiah; he had a strategy and a plan to back it up. Here is what he did. Half of the people with him worked on rebuilding the walls of Jerusalem while the other half protected them.

Here are a couple of questions I have for you: What are you going to say to the people and circumstances that come your way, conspiring to distract you from your greater purposes? Will you have the guts and grit to tell these people and the noise around you, "I'm doing important work, and I can't come down"? Nehemiah couldn't complete his work alone, and you probably won't be able to either. Who's got your back when you are doing the important work? Who is going to help you stick to the important work when you can't come down?

There was a valley nearby called Ono, but it is pronounced "Oh no." I'm not kidding. You couldn't make this stuff up. The people who came at Nehemiah wanted to do more than just distract him; they wanted to take him out. To do this they tried to get him off the wall and down to the "Oh no" valley. I'm willing to bet you've been to a place called "Oh no" in your life at some point. Perhaps you've listened to the cautious and fear-laced advice from the people around you. "What about this? *Oh no*. What about that? *Oh no*." You might feel like you are on the edge of this place, or perhaps you've been living there for a long time. Maybe you have fears born out of disappointments and letdowns in the past. Or anxiety about the future. Perhaps you are in the "Oh no" valley so often it feels like you should get a timeshare there and make it kind of like a lousy trip to Hawaii.

If you aren't in the "Oh no" valley now or haven't been there recently, I bet you know people who are the greeters. They are easy to spot because when a great idea comes their way, their first reaction is always: "Oh no. It'll never work. Why try? Give up! You're wasting your time. Be more realistic." These phrases are the coin of the realm for people in a constant state of "Oh no." Don't be one of them, and for Pete's sake, quit hanging out with people who are scaring you off the scent of your beautiful and lasting purpose. Remind yourself that *you are doing important work, and you're not going to come down.*

Find friends who have your back and keep you focused on the task at hand. We're not here to build consensus or a résumé; we're building a kingdom. Your life is not going to look like what everyone else wants their lives to look like. Find the cracks and holes in your wall, the places where you need to rebuild, strategize to stay on task, then curate a couple of friends who have your back while you do. Perform a distraction check every week. Call out the people and impediments getting you off track, then execute a self-care plan to stay the course. Decide in advance what you will do when distractions of every variety come your way. Have a process for refocusing yourself. Don't give any more airtime to the distractions around you. Remind yourself that you are doing important work and you will not, cannot, simply never will come down. That's how you build something that lasts. That's how you stay undistracted.

EPILOGUE

Thank you for coming along with me on the adventures in these pages. We have traveled quite a distance and crossed the finish line together. Unless, of course, you got distracted and left this book in your Uber ride or the seat pocket on an airplane. I hope you will look back at the parts of this book you underlined or dog-eared. If you made notes in the margins along the way, ask yourself why. Think for a moment about the journey you have made over the arc of this book. What stories resonated with you? Where did you see yourself in these pages? What ideas made sense to you? And in what area of your life did you decide to go ham?

Remember, mere agreement will change very little in your life; only action has the power to change everything for you. Stop thinking, planning, hand-wringing, and ruminating. Just start. Lists are for rookies; action is for the undistracted. If you are a planner, hatch a plan to live more deliberately, to be more present, and to cultivate the laser focus you may have lacked. Turn what has become water in your life back into wine.

As you try new things, don't be too hard on yourself, okay? Remember, God delights in you, and He made you to delight in

Him. A couple of things you try will work, and even more won't. The results aren't a vote up or down on your value, nor are they a referendum on your character. When the inevitable setbacks happen, lean in and learn; don't bail out and lament. Rather than abandon the pursuit, let go of the outcome and live into the newfound freedom that will accompany this change in approach. Decide in advance that your goal will be to influence your environment and the people in it without trying to control everything and everyone. Do these things, and you will become less distracted in your life.

Ann Landers famously said, "There are two kinds of people in this world. Those who walk into a room and say, 'Here I am' and those who walk into a room and say, 'There you are.'" Be the kind of person who says "There you are" to the people you meet. Make the time to take your busy schedule down a notch and notice what is happening around you and who is standing in front of you.

I know you have a lot going on. So do I. But before you become distracted by something else, I wanted to let you know how things turned out with some of my friends and circumstances mentioned in these chapters.

I'm still singing to Sweet Maria every morning, and she still groans and rolls over. I think she's secretly warming up to my songs. I have been back to Iraq quite a few more times, but I stick to the paved areas these days. The Oaks Retreat Center is packed wall-to-wall with amazing staff and participants each week, and we're all learning a ton. I haven't been bitten by a rattlesnake yet, but I'm still hoping. I never met the woman whose pacemaker stopped on my first visit there, but if I get a chance to meet her, I'll give her another kiss.

Ed is still playing lead guitar for Carrie Underwood and melting faces with his music. I am constantly reminding myself of the beautiful truth that I am already invited right up front to the big life Jesus talked about rather than settling for watching from afar. I hope you are too. I'm not going to take no for an answer anymore, but that doesn't mean I'll always take a yes. I'm duct-taping this reminder to my shirt every day.

I see Jesus in the room more than I did before. While I have fewer days in me than I once did, I still have enough to get into more of the right kind of mischief. My heart is beating strong and for the right things these days. I still get a lot of calls from the back of my books. I don't see these as interruptions or distractions, but invitations. Give me a call sometime. My cell number is (619) 985-4747.

I still go to San Quentin every month. These guys are amazing teachers, and I remain their student. We're learning to keep it real and consistent and finding freedom in these efforts. I'm also still flying but only in planes that are in better shape than the ones I have trusted in the past. I do my GUMPS check every time, and I have decided in advance that if there is another problem, I am going to level the wings, gain altitude, and fly the compass. Do the same and you'll get to your destination too.

I still have a couple of difficult people in my life, and I bet you have a couple in yours. I'm trying to burn the dry wood, not the green stuff anymore. I have a grandchild going into kindergarten soon and we'll see how long he lasts. Hopefully at least a day longer than I did. I'm still constantly asking myself where the stories in my life came from, what rules I scaffolded around the stories, and how I can find truer, more beautiful, and updated ones. While I do this I'm still asking Jesus to help my unbelief and holding on to Him wrist-to-wrist.

I'm a little more careful of whose car I get into at the airport. I'm spending less time studying Jesus and more time following Him, and I'm guarding my heart while I do this.

Jon and Lindsey had a son. Richard and Ashley had one too.

And Adam and Kaitlyn got married. It will not be the height of the family tree that matters, but the depth of its roots.

Efrim is still training fast horses to run faster, and Red keeps coming back to the barn to eat my carrots. The brown horse with the black tail had a foal, and we are training him to run fast. He will be easy for you to spot at the Kentucky Derby; he will be the one with balloons tied to him and a jockey of my size and hair color.

Bill is continuing with his courageous fight with cancer, and he's beating it with a stick. Laurie is still standing at his side and wields a pretty big stick too. Both of these people are made out of solid love.

Obomo graduated from law school and is getting ready to be a lawyer in Uganda. If you need some legal work done there, give someone else a call; we're still learning. We haven't dropped any more cameras by parachute into Congo, but we have built several schools. A volcano took one out. We were so mad about it, we built three more to replace it.

I'm watching the words I say these days, always mindful that I'm never shooting blanks and that some of my words are too costly. I still carry medals everywhere I go. I'm going to put one on the chest of the guy from Hawaii, and I'll save one for you, too, if you fail. It's not a billion-dollar check any of us need, but a nickel's worth of grace.

I still ride the horses and fall off now and then and return to the barn rather than chase them down. Like Pinocchio, I'm trying to become more real by being more brave, truthful, and unselfish. All it's going to take is twenty seconds of insane courage and a lifetime of practice.

You know enough about me from the stories I have shared with you to know that I have huge separation anxiety and don't like goodbyes. These are the remnants of the stories I have told myself over the years that people I love will leave me and not return. Something has changed inside of me, though, because I have rewritten the rules around this untrue story. I think we will be together for eternity, perhaps longer.

When Jesus was preparing to say goodbye to His friends, much like I'm preparing to do with you, He said this: "Peace I leave with you; my peace I give you. I do not give to you as the world gives. Do not let your hearts be troubled and do not be afraid."[1] Stated a little bit differently, find your peace with God, find your place in the world, do what it takes to be where your feet are. With everything you bring, with every last ounce of resolve within you, refuse to be distracted any longer.

See you at Tom Sawyer Island.

Bob

ACKNOWLEDGMENTS

Writing an acknowledgment is always a delight. It is like shooting up the last set of fireworks into the night sky in one last joyful celebration and finale in a book. Sweet Maria Goff, we did it. We finished another book. None of the words I wrote down would matter unless you were part of them.

It doesn't take a village to write a book, but it does take a wonderful family and a couple of dedicated friends. Thank you to Lindsey, Jon, Richard, Ashley, Adam, Kaitlyn, and a huge circle of friends for giving me a lifetime supply of support and stories to tell. You continue to be my teachers and guiding lights. Without your engaging spirits and the extravagant love you have sent my way, I am certain I would have continued to lead a thoroughly distracted life.

Thank you also to my dad who made my life possible and my dreams attainable. I love being your neighbor.

I'm grateful for the courageous Love Does team and its supporters around the world and to our students and staff in Afghanistan, Somalia, Uganda, Nepal, India, Uzbekistan, the DR Congo, the Dominican Republic, and Haiti. Your courageous leadership is going to change everything.

You all continue to release a truly stunning amount of love into the world.

To Stèphane, Brenda and your beautiful family, Bubba and Cindy, Kevin and Gwen, Tom, Stacey, and our family, and Michele Velcheck and her team, and the guys who have met with me on Friday mornings for decades. Many thanks to Rick Parker and for keeping my ticker going and also a special shout-out to the dock master at the Ala Wai Harbor for making one of my dreams possible.

I am indebted to Jody Luke who has been a constant and much needed support and encourager for decades and to the rest of the Love Does team, including Annie and Drew. Thank you also to the Bob Ink team who have kept the ship afloat by bailing it and me out when I have swamped it. Thank you, Becky Goodnight, Jordan Craig, Stephanie Wesson, Becca Phillips, Savannah Potafiy, Patrick Dodd, Scott Schimmel, John Richmond, and Tyler Wolford for your tireless work on my behalf. The countless people you interact with walk away feeling loved because you are so good at it.

Many thanks also to my friends and coconspirators Kim Stewart, Taylor Hughes, Megan Tibbits, and Jay Desai. It has been a unique delight to travel on buses, tag along behind you, and carry your books, bags of tricks, and instruments as you have released unreasonable amounts of hope and joy into the world using your immense gifts.

A project like this also takes an unflappable publishing team to get a book over the finish line. Thank you to the entire team at Thomas Nelson who worked to get these words into print even when I was terribly late. A huge thank you to Tim Paulson, Stephanie Tresner, Kristen Golden, Jennifer Smith, Janene MacIvor, Claire Drake, Daniel Marrs, Rachel Tockstein, and the team at Process Creative and Richard Goff for the cover design.

A special shout-out to Bryan Norman who has been my wing man on every book and once again made all my words better. If books had pastors, I would be in your congregation. You are a gentle giant, ridiculously talented, and generous with your time and input. You love God and have been the heartbeat behind every book I have ever written. Your fingerprints are like a watermark existing on every page of this book, and your friendship has helped me understand more about my own faith.

I also have gained a huge amount of perspective from the team at The Oaks retreat center and our equestrian program. Thank you Miles and Venessa Adcox as well as Jamie Kern Lima and Paulo Lima for dreaming this place into existence. And thank you for the team that puts legs on the love at The Oaks. Adam and Kaitlyn Goff, Sweet Maria, Justin, Stefanie and Ellie Boyce, Annie Bishop, Maggie Garrett, Jeremy Ward, Avery Wringlever, Darcy Murillo, Ben Love, and our culinary team led by Jessica Slama. For Darrell Norman and Mago Santiago, Holly Anderson, Heidi Pullen, two friends named Efrim and Reuben, and everyone who makes the beds and sets the vibe.

Without each of your unique contributions to my life, this book would not have happened.

NOTES

Chapter 2: The Keyhole of Eternity
1. 2 Corinthians 3:2–3.
2. James 4:14.

Chapter 3: Breaking Free by Coming Home
1. Romans 7:15.

Chapter 4: The Happiness of Pursuit
1. 2 Corinthians 12:10; 1 Timothy 6:6–7.
2. 2 Timothy 1:6.

Chapter 6: All-Access Pass
1. Luke 23:49.
2. Tuan C. Nguyen, "A Short History of Duct Tape," July 30, 2019, thoughtco.com, https://www.thoughtco.com/history-of-duct -tape-4040012.
3. "A Short History of Duct Tape," Tuan C. Nguyen, https://www .thoughtco.com/history-of-duct-tape-4040012.

Chapter 7: Jesus in the Room
1. Matthew 6:11.
2. 1 Corinthians 13:13.
3. Mark 14:66–72.
4. Luke 2:41–52.
5. John 2:1–11.
6. Luke 23:32–43 (Jesus, the criminals, and the crucifixion);

John 20:13–18 (Mary at the tomb); Luke 24:13–35 (Emmaus road); John 21:4 (shoreline).
7. Matthew 18:20.
8. "The Average Person Lives 27,375 Days. Make Each of Them Count," blog, JoshuaKennon.com, https://www.joshuakennon.com/the-average-person-lives-27375-days-make-each-of-them-count/.

Chapter 8: No Stalking, Please
1. Proverbs 4:23.

Chapter 9: Tooth Fairies and Shrinking Airplanes
1. "Kid Logic (2016)," December 16, 2016, https://www.thisamericanlife.org/605/kid-logic-2016.
2. Mark 9:24.
3. Hebrews 11:1.
4. Matthew 14:28–29.
5. Matthew 14:15–21.
6. Matthew 8:23–27.
7. Original reads: "God whispers to us in our pleasures, speaks in our conscience, but shouts in our pain," C. S. Lewis, *The Problem of Pain* (1940; repr., San Francisco: HarperSanFrancisco, 2001), 91.
8. James 5:14.

Chapter 10: Count Yourself Among the Stars
1. Matthew 26:39.
2. John 19:30.

Chapter 11: "Cease Fire!"
1. Luke 6:45.

Chapter 12: The Wrong Button
1. Benjamin Hardy, PhD, "23 Michael Jordan Quotes That Will Immediately Boost Your Confidence," Inc.com, https://www.inc.com/benjamin-p-hardy/23-michael-jordan-quotes-that-will-immediately-boost-your-confidence.html.

Chapter 13: Pinocchio's Nose

1. Acts 5:1–11.
2. "Whatever Happened to Pavlov's Dogs?" Headspace, October 23, 2013, https://phdheadspace.wordpress.com/2013/10/23/what-ever-happened-to-pavlovs-dogs/.

Chapter 14: The Misadventures of a Serial Reject

1. "Puritanism," Chesterton in Brief, accessed November 8, 2021, https://www.chesterton.org/puritanism/.
2. Steve Wright, https://www.goodreads.com/quotes/146279-experience-is-something-you-don-t-get-until-just-after-you.

Chapter 15: Stop Chasing the Horse

1. Matt Damon in *We Bought a Zoo*, directed by Cameron Crowe (Los Angeles: 20th Century Fox, 2011).
2. Hebrews 12:1.

Chapter 16: Driven Out of the Shallows

1. Annie Dillard, *The Writing Life* (New York: Harper Perennial, 2013), 68.

Chapter 17: "Oh my gosh!"

1. John 17:4.

Chapter 18: Five Minutes from Now

1. Colossians 3:23.

Epilogue

1. John 14:27.

ABOUT THE AUTHOR

Bob is the longest-serving volunteer at Love Does and is its chief balloon inflator. He calls himself a "recovering lawyer" because after practicing law for almost thirty years, he walked into his own law firm and quit in order to pursue encouraging people full time. Bob is driven by a desire to love people and to motivate others to do the same. These days, you'll find Bob in an airport on his way to connect with and encourage people or, more likely, on his way home for supper with Sweet Maria.

A few years ago, Bob wrote a book called *Everybody, Always.* Before that, he wrote one called *Love Does.* He gave away all the proceeds from that book to help change the lives of children in countries where armed conflicts had left them vulnerable. Today, Love Does is an organization dedicated to helping kids in these areas, including Uganda, Somalia, Afghanistan, Nepal, and India. You can find out more about Love Does at www.LoveDoes.org.

CONNECT WITH BOB

Bob's passion is people. He'd love to hear from you if you want to email him at info@bobgoff.com. You can also follow him on Instagram and Twitter, @bobgoff.

Here's his cell phone number if you want to give him a call: (619) 985-4747.

Bob is a personal coach. If you're interested, you can find out more at coachingwithbobgoff.com. He is also available to inspire and engage your team, organization, or audience. To date, he's spoken to more than two million people, bringing his unique perspective and exciting storytelling with him. If you're interested in having Bob come to your event, check out bobgoff.com/invite.

Beloved and *New York Times* bestselling author Bob Goff provides you with a year's worth of inspiring, unexpected, humble teaching on grace and love that will prepare you for the day ahead.

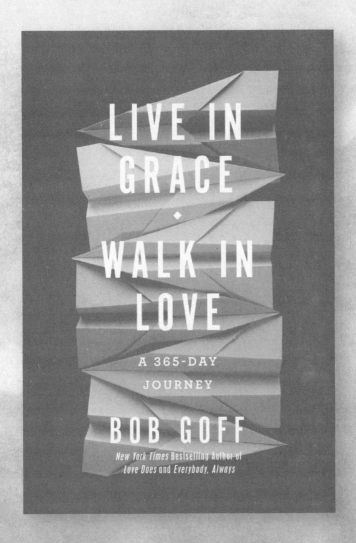